# Migration:
# A World History

The New Oxford World History

# Migration: A World History

Michael H. Fisher

OXFORD
UNIVERSITY PRESS

# OXFORD
UNIVERSITY PRESS

Oxford University Press is a department of the University of Oxford.
It furthers the University's objective of excellence in research,
scholarship, and education by publishing worldwide.

Oxford   New York
Auckland   Cape Town   Dar es Salaam   Hong Kong   Karachi
Kuala Lumpur   Madrid   Melbourne   Mexico City   Nairobi
New Delhi   Shanghai   Taipei   Toronto

With offices in
Argentina   Austria   Brazil   Chile   Czech Republic   France   Greece
Guatemala   Hungary   Italy   Japan   Poland   Portugal   Singapore
South Korea   Switzerland   Thailand   Turkey   Ukraine   Vietnam

Oxford is a registered trade mark of Oxford University Press
in the UK and certain other countries.

Published in the United States of America by
Oxford University Press
198 Madison Avenue, New York, NY 10016

© 2014 by Oxford University Press

Library of Congress Cataloging-in-Publication Data
Fisher, Michael Herbert
New Oxford world history : a world history / Michael H. Fisher.
pages   cm
Includes bibliographical references and index.
ISBN 978-0-19-976433-4 (pbk.)—ISBN 978-0-19-976434-1 (hbk.)
1. Emigration and immigration—History. 2. Migration, Internal—History. I. Title.
JV6021.F54   2013
304.809—dc23   2013037096

*Frontispiece: Each Gold Rush attracted immigrants seeking a quick fortune, although not all arrived and few returned rich. This 1898 photograph of "women prospectors on their way to Klondike" shows some of the 100,000 Gold Rush immigrants to Yukon territory, Canada, trudging through freezing mud, past a row of saloons and hotels.* Photo by Benjamin West, courtesy Library of Congress Prints and Photographs Division, LC-USZ62-2129

*To my greatest support and toughest critic*

# Contents

# Editors' Preface

This book is part of the New Oxford World History, an innovative series that offers readers an informed, lively, and up-to-date history of the world and its people that represents a significant change from the "old" world history. Only a few years ago, world history generally amounted to a history of the West—Europe and the United States—with small amounts of information from the rest of the world. Some versions of the "old" world history drew attention to every part of the world *except* Europe and the United States. Readers of that kind of world history could get the impression that somehow the rest of the world was made up of exotic people who had strange customs and spoke difficult languages. Still another kind of "old" world history presented the story of areas or peoples of the world by focusing primarily on the achievements of great civilizations. One learned of great buildings, influential world religions, and mighty rulers but little of ordinary people or more general economic and social patterns. Interactions among the world's peoples were often told from only one perspective.

This series tells world history differently. First, it is comprehensive, covering all countries and regions of the world and investigating the total human experience—even those of so-called peoples without histories living far from the great civilizations. "New" world historians thus share in common an interest in all of human history, even going back millions of years before there were written human records. A few "new" world histories even extend their focus to the entire universe, a "big history" perspective that dramatically shifts the beginning of the story back to the big bang. Some see the "new" global framework of world history today as viewing the world from the vantage point of the Moon, as one scholar put it. We agree. But we also want to take a close-up view, analyzing and reconstructing the significant experiences of all of humanity.

This is not to say that everything that has happened everywhere and in all time periods can be recovered or is worth knowing, but that there is much to be gained by considering both the separate and interrelated stories of different societies and cultures. Making these connections is still another crucial ingredient of the "new" world history. It emphasizes connectedness and interactions of all kinds—cultural, economic, political, religious, and social—involving peoples, places, and processes. It makes comparisons and finds similarities. Emphasizing both the comparisons and interactions is critical to developing a global framework that can deepen and broaden historical understanding, whether the focus is on a specific country or region or on the whole world.

The rise of the new world history as a discipline comes at an opportune time. The interest in world history in schools and among the general public is vast. We travel to one another's nations, converse and work with people around the world, and are changed by global events. War and peace affect populations worldwide as do economic conditions and the state of our environment, communications, and health and medicine. The New Oxford World History presents local histories in a global context and gives an overview of world events seen through the eyes of ordinary people. This combination of the local and the global further defines the new world history. Understanding the workings of global and local conditions in the past gives us tools for examining our own world and for envisioning the interconnected future that is in the making.

Bonnie G. Smith
Anand Yang

# Preface: Migration in World History and as World History

Around 1002 CE, an immigrant from Iceland, Gudrid "the Traveler," settled in eastern Canada and gave birth to a son, Snorri. According to Norse oral tradition, she was "of striking appearance and wise."[1] To reach her new home, she had traveled 3,000 miles in small Viking sailing and rowing vessels across the stormy north Atlantic. Because Gudrid's native Iceland had been first populated by Scandinavian men and their mainly Irish or Scottish wives, her recent ancestors probably came from several lands.

Gudrid had first immigrated to the Scandinavian colonies on Greenland. Widowed, she had remarried with a recent immigrant from Norway, Thorfinn Karlsefn. Once having emigrated, people are more willing to do so again. So Gudrid and her husband soon set out with a few dozen followers for the region they called Vinland, which had been recently visited by her brother-in-law, Leif Erikson. From her new homestead, she occasionally traded cow's milk and woven cloth for furs brought by nomadic hunting and fishing Amerindians. Evidence of these exchanges was discovered in 1960 at Gudrid's homestead site at L'Anse aux Meadows, Newfoundland.

Amerindians had also recently immigrated into the area, their ancestors having walked eastward from Asia over the Bering Strait to Alaska, then 4,000 miles across Canada to the Atlantic. Because America contained no cattle that could be domesticated and milked and because these Amerindians did not weave cloth, they welcomed Gudrid's goods. Their furs from unfamiliar American animals were highly valued by Gudrid and the other Scandinavians.

Many migrations involve conflicts, however. After sporadic hostilities with these Amerindians, Gudrid and her companions departed and, in a return-migration, sailed back to Greenland. Later, she moved to Iceland and then probably on to Norway. However brief these encounters between Amerindians and Scandinavians were, human migrations had encircled the globe.

*Gudrid and her Scandinavian companions, the first immigrants from Europe to settle in North America around 1000 CE, built a sod-covered homestead in the region they called Vinland. Using archaeological evidence, Parks Canada has reconstructed a replica on the site in L'Anse aux Meadows, Newfoundland.* Photo courtesy David Sexton

We are all the descendants of migrants and we virtually all migrate during the course of our own lives. From the origin of our Homo sapiens species about 200,000 BCE until today, we have expanded our range over the entire planet. We have emigrated to seek new opportunities, often driven out by deteriorating social or physical environments. As the earth's climate has changed and our societies have developed, migration has enabled us to better our lives and those of our children.

Over the course of world history, we have gradually invented new technologies that have accelerated our migrations, including domesticating horses, creating new kinds of ships, and building airplanes. We have equipped ourselves to be able to live in almost any environment and have altered the earth to satisfy our needs and wants. But migration when the world was relatively empty of people clearly differed from now when there are over seven billion of us. Increasingly, over time, immigrants have had to adapt to or expel communities already living there.

Many migrations have been peaceful, but others have been violent. Indeed, wars have caused many of the largest mass migrations throughout history. Soldiers from invading armies occupy conquered lands, while people already living there often flee as refugees, many never to return. Environmental degradation caused by humans, as well as natural disasters, have made once fruitful lands uninhabitable and have led to whole communities emigrating as ecological refugees.

Over centuries, states have created technologies that block or control migrations. The earliest rulers built defensive walls to keep other people out. Later governments have created policed borders that require official passports and other forms of documentation of legal identities. Today, virtually all of the earth's land has been claimed by one or more of the world's nearly two hundred national governments.

While larger migration patterns describe groups and communities, each individual has a unique life history of migration, be it local or to a distant continent. Some people spend much of their lives migrating, as seasonal workers or by following a nomadic way of life. But each of us migrates to at least some degree, moving to a new place to marry or divorce, or pursuing new opportunities by going off for education, pilgrimage, adventure, community or military service, or other work. Very few people remain in their parents' home throughout life, never spending any significant time away. From the earliest Homo sapiens to all of us today, migration, in its many forms, has remained central to world history.

## CHAPTER I

# Earliest Human Migrations, ca. 200,000 BCE to ca. 600 CE

Sometime between 3300 and 3150 BCE, during the early summer, forty-six-year-old "Ötzi the Iceman" climbed through a mountain pass in the Tyrolean Alps (now on the Italian-Austrian border). He was well equipped as a traveler, migrating hunter, or herder. But he was violently killed among the rocks. Alpine winds immediately froze his body and then an expanding glacier entombed him. More than fifty centuries later, in 1991, after global warming melted his ice tomb, climbers discovered him. His body and equipage were moved to the South Tyrol Archaeological Museum in Bolzano, Italy, where scientists have been using the latest methods to analyze his migrations.[1]

Ötzi's body was shaped by genes from each parent and composed of the foods that he consumed; their origins show ancestral and personal migration patterns. Each person's DNA (deoxyribonucleic acid) has an individual set of chromosomes, largely fixed at the moment of conception and formed from the combination of both parents' genomes: the Y-chromosome only descends in the male lineage from father to son while mitochondrial DNA (mtDNA) comes only from the mother. These sexually distinct genetic inheritances can trace a person's ancestry separately through male and female lines. Ötzi has the oldest human DNA yet analyzed, indicating that his father and mother each shared genes with other people who moved from northeast Africa into west Asia and then into central Europe. But his particular paternal and maternal lineages are both very rare today, and he appears to be not closely related to any current Europeans.

Ötzi's physical skeleton also contains chemical evidence about where he migrated. Food in every region has a distinctive chemical composition, including rare elements and isotopes in unique proportions.

We incorporate these at different life stages as we eat and as our bodies develop. During Ötzi's youth, he formed tooth enamel in one valley but later he moved to another valley where he lived at least a decade before he was killed. The food, ornaments, attire, and artifacts that Ötzi carried with him reveal much about the particular cultures of his own community and those with which it traded and fought.

Undigested food in his stomach shows the animals he hunted and the kinds of grain that his community grew or obtained, including einkorn, a kind of wheat not originally native to Europe. Ötzi had fifty short lines tattooed over his arms, back, and legs; their meaning is yet unexplained—like many tattoos today they were perhaps a personal choice or his community's custom. His clothing included the tanned skins of domesticated goats sewn together to make various garments: a calfskin belt, deerskin laces and shoe-uppers, and a bearskin cap and shoe soles. His leather pouch contained flint and tinder for making fire. The four-inch-long ax head he bore was of nearly pure copper, which had to be imported from afar. The dagger he carried had a five-inch-long flint that came from the Lessini Mountains, near Verona, 150 miles away. His arrows and other gear had bloodstains from four other people. He himself had an arrowhead in his left shoulder and had received a blow to his head: he lived, migrated, and died with violence. The plant pollen and leaves and fruits found with him indicate the early summer season of his death. Like Ötzi, each of us carries in our body and in our culture evidence of human migrations.

Our own genes come from our hominid ancestors who evolved in Africa at least five to six million years ago, with a major defining physical feature being bipedalism, or the ability to walk efficiently on two legs. Eventually, hominids enhanced their capacity to migrate by inventing tools they could carry with them. They also discovered how to transport and then create fire for cooking food, providing warmth during cool nights, scaring off more powerful predators, and clearing undergrowth in the forests. Various branches of hominids used these physical and cultural achievements in order to spread out over Africa and much of Eurasia by 1.5 million years ago. Migration has always been central to human identity.

Our own distinct hominid species, Homo sapiens, evolved in Africa as physically modern human beings only about 200,000 years ago. Subsequent human genetic evolution has been relatively limited compared to those early fundamental changes. So, we are all the same human species, despite superficial differences among groups of people.

Along with our unique biology, Homo sapiens also have a distinctive cognitive capacity that distinguishes us from all other creatures, including other hominids. About 100,000 years ago, when Homo sapiens migrated within Africa, we began to develop the complex languages, social organization, and technological innovations that mark us as "culturally modern" human beings, unique among hominids. As a consequence of our longest history within Africa, that continent today contains the greatest concentration of human genetic and linguistic diversity: some 2,000 surviving ethnicities and 30 percent of the world's distinct languages.

South Africa's Blombos Cave holds incised red ochre stone and other minerals, beads, bone tools, and decorated eggshells dating from 70,000 years ago. Archaeologists have also discovered early human-made artistic representations in several other African regions, showing how particular technologies and ideas migrated among human populations or were independently invented. In what is today Namibia, drawings on the walls of caves from 27,000 to 23,000 BCE illustrate recognizable

*About 100,000 years ago, Homo sapiens began to express our cognitive capacity by producing not just tools but also abstract representations of the world. This photograph shows sharp stone points, bone tools, and a smoothed face of a piece of ochre (soft red stone containing iron) with carved geometric patterns dating from about 70,000 years ago, preserved in Blombos Cave, east of today's Cape Town, South Africa, on the shore of the Indian Ocean.* Photo courtesy Chris Henshilwood

animals. In today's Algeria, pottery representing humans and animals dates from about 20,000 BCE. In the Sahara from about 8500 BCE (during one of its wet phases), rock paintings show humans hunting the hippopotamus and other water-loving creatures. All this art begins to reveal how different communities of Homo sapiens perceived themselves and the other hominids and animals they moved among.

Due to endemic diseases and other environmental challenges, early populations of Homo sapiens in Africa remained small and lived in widely scattered nomadic groups. These hunting, foraging, and fishing ways of life produced seasonal food supplies but little could be stored for very long or transported by foot. To reconstruct our earliest communities, anthropologists have studied dozens of small bands that live today as hunter-foragers, such as the Khoisan (Bushmen) of the Kalahari Desert in South Africa and the Ache of Paraguay's jungles. We should not assume that Homo sapiens of 200,000 to 100,000 years ago lived exactly like today's hunting-foraging communities but, based on such evidence, it appears that early Homo sapiens organized their bands with complementary roles determined by age, gender, and individual capacity, but with little other internal differentiation.

These early communities were dynamic and mobile. Bands merged as conditions changed. Individuals migrated between bands, conveying new skills and environmental knowledge and avoiding incest. As people moved off in pairs or small groups, they formed new bands, becoming founders of new genetic and cultural descent lines. Bands competed but also exchanged valuable materials, including surplus food, raw stone suitable for chipping spearheads, and finished artifacts.

Despite the advantages of collective hunting and social life, only small populations could be supported by any single region. Bands, therefore, frequently migrated for short or long distances, on foot or using simple watercraft like dug-out canoes or bamboo, wooden, or reed rafts, depending on the materials available. Bands might return to favored sites, either seasonally or after a generation or more, but did not seem to have resided in permanent locations. Throughout history, most Homo sapiens have continued to migrate to unknown areas in search of new opportunities.

Over the course of human existence, long phases of global warming and cooling have caused drying or wetting of individual regions, the expanding and retreating of glaciers, and the falling and rising of seas. The physical and cultural hunting abilities of early Homo sapiens enabled them to adapt especially well to the planet's changing climate, as when cooling and drying phases changed heavy forests to open savannah. When regions became too dry to support much animal or plant life, Homo sapiens emigrated to more fertile areas. Thus, climate change has been a recurrent cause for human migration.

From about 60,000 to 70,000 years ago, early Homo sapiens extended their range to include lands beyond Africa. Northeast Africa is connected by a land bridge to the Sinai peninsula and then to the northern Arabian peninsula and west Asia; additionally, the water passage from the Horn of Africa to the Arabian peninsula's southwest corner was in some geological eras even narrower than today. So, as had other hominids long before, bands of Homo sapiens following herds or fishing or seeking other food occasionally walked or paddled beyond Africa. Many emigrant bands may not have survived or may have returned to Africa, but some eventually established themselves in Eurasia.

Today's perception of Africa as a separate continent reveals the dramatic significance in world history of this first successful intercontinental migration by Homo sapiens. But Africa's earliest emigrants probably experienced their entry into Eurasia as only a continuation of their long-established nomadic way of life. Gradually, they discovered that there were many natural resources and no rival Homo sapiens ahead of them. Throughout human history, people have continued to migrate out of Africa, but current genetic evidence suggests that these early emigrant bands were small and that most people in Eurasia and the Americas today are descended from these early female and male emigrants.

These immigrants spread out unevenly across Eurasia, channeled by geological features including mountains, rivers, seashores, and climatic zones. These bands hunted, foraged, and fished as opportunities offered. Some streams of Homo sapiens flowed eastward along the warm and productive coasts of the Indian Ocean to southeast Asia. Other communities of Homo sapiens spread north along the eastern Mediterranean shore into Asia and eventually into Europe. By about 40,000 years ago, Homo sapiens had extended across all the habitable areas of Africa and Eurasia.

Walking or paddling simple watercraft to cover the 5,000 miles from northeast Africa to the western Pacific may seem daunting. But pairs or groups of people moving only about forty miles away from their parents would mean Homo sapiens would extend over the entire distance in 2,500 years (calculating twenty years per average generation). Many bands roved much further during one person's lifetime. Expansion across Eurasia took many generations but was remarkably quick in terms of world history.

These diverse new lands did not contain the endemic human diseases that had infected people in Africa. Also, the colder winters in northern Eurasia cut down on pathogenic parasites that people had long carried with them. As healthier Homo sapiens invented ways to use the many new plants, animals, and minerals available, populations in particularly abundant areas of Eurasia expanded quickly. But when local conditions declined, as they did periodically, people emigrated outward— such regions formed population pumps. As Homo sapiens spread out, distantly separated communities developed distinctive cultural and physical features.

Roughly 45,000 years ago, related communities of Homo sapiens in southwest Eurasia developed a cluster of empowering technologies (called Aurignacian after the site in France where such evidence was first identified). Using a two-stage technique, they first prepared a rock core from which they could then more efficiently flake off large numbers of thin, sharp blades used for hunting and preparing foods. These and other groups across Eurasia also began to use animal bones, ivory, antlers, and other materials to make shelters, fishhooks, and spearheads and to fashion needles for sewn clothing. These new tools led to further population growth and outward-spreading migrations. Scientists continue to debate how much Homo sapiens interacted with other hominid species, such as Neanderthals, during the long period of living among them, including how much the two species interbred, which human tools and other cultural products were used or even invented by Neanderthals, and if Homo sapiens exterminated or simply out-survived them by adapting better to changes in the earth's climate.

The last major ice age peaked around 20,000 to 15,000 BCE, with the northern part of the globe covered by forbidding glaciers. But these glaciers also locked up vast amounts of water, which lowered the world's sea level some 350 feet, thus temporarily extending the shoreline outward from each continent and narrowing water passages between them. Newly exposed lands temporarily merged mainland Southeast Asia with surrounding islands, including Sumatra, Java, and Borneo; scholars call this temporary landmass Sunda. Beyond a strait of fifty to sixty miles (at its narrowest) lay merged New Guinea and Australia, a temporary landmass called Sahul.

Homo sapiens walked across the temporary continent of Sunda and propelled watercraft around its coast as well as crossed the narrowed sea passage to the temporary continent of Sahul. When the glaciers melted and the oceans rose, Sunda and Sahul separated into mainland Southeast Asia and many islands. Some communities were isolated in the resulting low islands, the fertile valleys of high islands, and also ecological niches in Australia, producing the great cultural diversity still

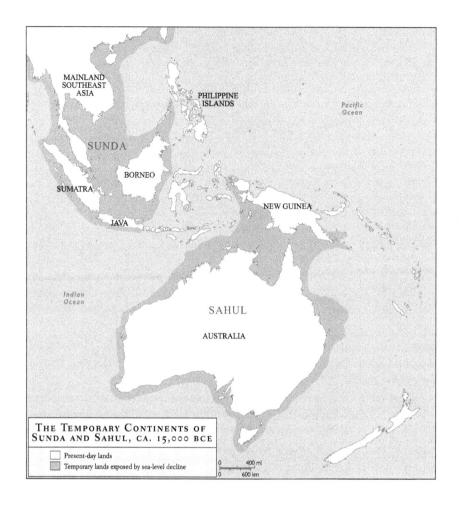

THE TEMPORARY CONTINENTS OF
SUNDA AND SAHUL, CA. 15,000 BCE

☐ Present-day lands
▨ Temporary lands exposed by sea-level decline

found there. New Guinea today contains some 800 Papuan languages and Australia some 240 aboriginal languages.

By 15,000 BCE, bands of Homo sapiens had also migrated into North America over a 600-mile-wide land bridge between Siberia and Alaska called Beringia, exposed by the same lowering sea level. Northern Siberia and northern America shared similar icy climates, allowing these migrants to pass relatively easily back and forth between continents over this temporarily uncovered bridge and also by sea over the narrowed strait, both before and after Beringia's surfacing. Other hominids had evidently never established themselves in the Americas; they may have been unable to adapt to the harsh Alaskan environment. But as glaciers melted, the land passage across Beringia was

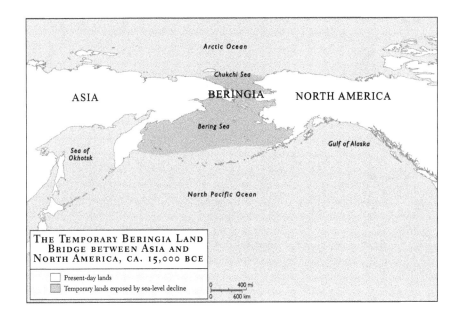

THE TEMPORARY BERINGIA LAND
BRIDGE BETWEEN ASIA AND
NORTH AMERICA, CA. 15,000 BCE

☐ Present-day lands
▨ Temporary lands exposed by sea-level decline

again submerged, separating Eurasia and North America. Homo sapiens expanded from Alaska along ice-free corridors into the rest of North America.

Over time, different streams of Homo sapiens extended south along North America's Pacific coast, into America's Great Plains, its forested eastern seaboard, and into Central and South America. Other bands migrated east across Canada as far as Greenland. By 12,800 BCE, Amerindians had reached Patagonia in southern Chile, at the tip of South America, more than 11,000 miles from Alaska.

As people spread across the diverse climates of the Americas, their cultures differentiated. In order to reconstruct the complex patterns of human migration in the Americas, geneticists have traced Amerindian male and female descent lines from Asians and also mutations that evidently occurred only after immigration into the Americas. Linguists have identified more than 600 languages that first emerged in North America. By about 10,000 BCE, the beginning of the geological Holocene Era, Homo sapiens ranged across Africa, Eurasia, Australia, and the Americas, with only a few lands left uninhabited, including Greenland, Madagascar, and New Zealand.

In different world regions, various nomadic communities on different continents independently learned how to capture, rear, and tame local animal species to eat, help them hunt or herd, or carry loads or ride. Among the earliest domesticated animals were dogs (about 13,000 BCE),

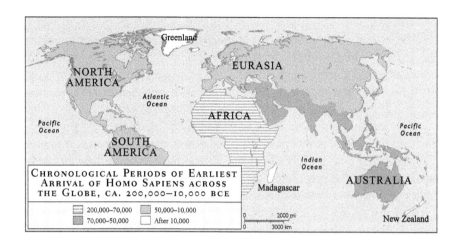

CHRONOLOGICAL PERIODS OF EARLIEST ARRIVAL OF HOMO SAPIENS ACROSS THE GLOBE, CA. 200,000–10,000 BCE

200,000–70,000  50,000–10,000
70,000–50,000  After 10,000

then goats, sheep, pigs, cats, cattle, chickens, and horses (by about 3,000 BCE), followed by llamas, alpacas, camels, water buffaloes, yaks, and donkeys. Over time, human communities have selectively bred these animals; today's dog breeds vary widely but all originated from a single species of wolf. Many communities built their way of life around tending and migrating their domesticated animals.

While many groups still follow predominantly nomadic ways of life, over the course of world history ever more people began to settle in fixed locations. And, while "nomadic" and "settled" are useful categories, each represents a range of ways of life. Various individuals and whole communities have shifted back and forth between these categories as conditions or inclination motivated. Nomadic and settled groups have often conflicted, but they have also often supported each other, exchanging people and complementary goods and services. However, nomadic and settled people have always had different patterns of migration.

From the beginning of Homo sapiens, nomadic communities have almost always combined foraging of wild plants with hunting and fishing, but in different proportions as enabled by the local environment and their own technologies. In some regions, bands practiced transhumant migration, moving seasonally back and forth between nearby but different climatic zones in order to use the plants they found or grew in each. Many forest-dwelling communities developed a migratory farming practice called swidden, where they burned the undergrowth to clear land for crops and, when that site's soil became exhausted after a season or a few years, shifted to a new area, perhaps eventually returning to earlier sites. Many scholars believe these practices created transitions to permanent settlement.

As Homo sapiens spread over the globe, a few communities discovered locations so abundant in plants or animals that they could settle there for hundreds of years. Archaeologists have found such longstanding settlements dating from 13,000 BCE in geographically distant sites, including the Natufian people along the eastern Mediterranean coast and the Jomon people on Honshu, Japan's largest island.

The Jomon people made impressive pots to store their surplus food and imprinted distinctive patterns of cords on the clay when it was soft. The emergence of pottery often marks permanent settlement because, while valuable for preserving grains and other produce, pottery can be bulky and heavy to transport by land. Communities in Eurasia, Africa, and the Americas independently invented pottery, each creating their own customary shapes and sizes. Specific communities used distinctive techniques of shaping the clay, including using hands, paddles, baskets woven from reeds or twigs, or throwing wheels. Some then applied specific decorative patterns with characteristic surface markings and glazes. They then dried or fired them in particular ways. Since potsherds and other artifacts made of fired clay tend to last and since customs within a community tend to change only over long historical phases, archaeologists can use these durable artifacts to learn much about their makers and trading partners over time.

Similarly, evidence about other technological innovations has been preserved through stone tools and other imperishable materials. Communities of Amerindians invented distinctive arrowheads from about 11,500 BCE, as their skills developed in ways of chipping stones to create weapons with sharpened edges and a beveled base for inserting in a shaft. Since Amerindians were isolated from Eurasia and Africa, similar types of stone tools dating from roughly 12,000 BCE found around the globe show that several human cultures independently developed a Neolithic Revolution. Neolithic stone-working crafts are associated with a range of new cultural developments and farming methods that had substantial benefits for settled and nomadic communities. For instance, polished and ground stone artifacts aided in hunting, skinning animals, and warfare, and multiple small sharpened stone flakes attached to shafts created scythes for cutting stalks of wild grains or other grasses.

Cultures around the world, from 7000 to 1500 BCE, discovered or learned from immigrants or neighbors how to use metals to produce weapons, tools, ornaments, and other artifacts. The techniques of mining, smelting, refining, and working various metals, including copper, gold, silver, bronze (made from copper and tin), and iron, required imagination, experience, and intense work. Nomadic and settled communities

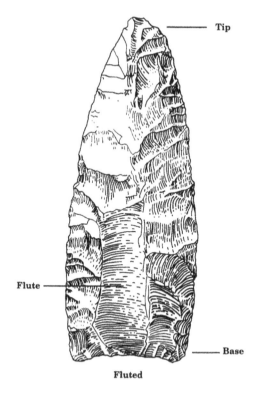

Tip

Flute

Base

Fluted

*Particular communities of Homo sapiens developed distinctive technologies to produce tools and other artifacts that sometimes spread widely as people migrated and traded. One especially effective type of arrowhead created in North America is called the "Clovis point" after the site in New Mexico where it was first identified.* Courtesy U.S. Department of the Interior, Bureau of Land Management

usually participated differently in the production and use of metals. For example, nomads often carried ore that they traded for finished articles made from that ore by settled communities.

Several cultures separately invented the wheel from as early as 3500 BCE. Wheels on axles greatly assisted both nomadic migration and also transportation within settled communities, wherever the ground was suitable and wherever people could domesticate animals to pull carts, wagons, or chariots. However, some means of transportation widely used in Eurasia were unavailable in the Americas. Bison, elk, and deer in North America and llamas and alpacas in South America's Andes Mountains proved valuable for food and clothing but could not be ridden, heavily loaded as pack animals, or used to pull plows or wheeled carts. Major parts of sub-Saharan Africa were unhealthy for horses and other draft animals due to diseases and climate. Thus, these communities could not use the wheel for transportation; walking or paddling limited the volume and weight of material possessions they could carry. Nonetheless, in many lands, nomads carried artifacts and valuable, low-volume raw materials long distances and traded with each other and with settled farming communities.

Globally, people living near bodies of water developed skills in producing watercraft suitable for their needs from available materials. Reeds and logs could be simply bound together as rafts. Wooden frames covered by skins or bark produced light but sturdy boats. Several cultures around the world independently invented the sail from about 3000 BCE. Sailing meant vessels needed fewer oarsmen and could carry more families, provisions, plants, and animals necessary to settle uninhabited lands.

Using innovative single- and multi-hulled outrigger vessels, powered by efficient sails, families from Southeast Asia and Taiwan migrated throughout the far-flung islands of the Pacific. These Polynesians also developed sophisticated navigation skills that enabled them to cross long distances, even reaching previously unknown islands by reading patterns in the waves and sky. By 1000 BCE, Polynesians had populated most of the islands of western Micronesia and Melanesia and also voyaged west across the Indian Ocean to Madagascar. By 500 CE, they had migrated to most Pacific islands (although New Zealand would not be permanently settled until about 1200 CE). Settlers on each island brought new flora and fauna and developed distinctive cultures, including languages.

Fostered by both global environmental warming and cultural developments, including Neolithic technologies, various communities around the world became more settled as they independently discovered how to domesticate regionally available plant species, including grains, tubers, and fruits. In Eurasia, Africa, and the Americas during the Agricultural Revolution from 12,000 to 1500 BCE, communities invented methods of farming, which were then spread by emigrants. Farming, as a way of life, could support a larger and far denser population than could a nomadic life of hunting, fishing, or foraging. Hence, settled communities developed villages, some of which eventually grew into towns and cities. However, there were also negative health consequences to settlements: contagious diseases thrive more readily in a concentrated population; diets high in starches can produce vitamin deficiencies, caries, and other physical ailments. Farming also requires more work than does a nomadic way of life and tends to create inequalities within the community.

As settled communities grew larger, their stored food surplus and need for complex tools, techniques, and economic organization correlated with new social differentiation. These societies also developed new patterns of migration within and between them. Farming meant an even greater division and redistribution of labor because many farmers needed seasonal workers to plant and harvest and artisans to produce tools. Emerging rulers used coercion and culture, including religion, to order the society beneath them—demanding taxes, service, and obedience. In many settled societies around the world, elders (patriarchs or, more rarely, matriarchs) took leadership roles collectively as councils or individually as chiefs or monarchs, often claiming divine sanction for their authority. Rulers also promised both to protect their people from outsiders (both nomads and other settled communities) and to conquer others.

Farmers devoted time, energy, and emotional commitment to immovable fields, wells, canals, and houses; to heavy and bulky tools like grinding stones and pottery; and to their stored harvests. Thus, while nomads could easily move away or break off from the group, farmers were generally more reluctant to cut their bonds to their community and their land, even when drought or other natural disasters occurred, or when powerful community leaders demanded some of their crops, labor, or children. Nonetheless, individuals in farming communities migrated within and beyond them. Brides and grooms moved between households. Many thriving communities extended their frontiers or hived off colonies. Young men and women served in expanding administrations, armies, and building projects that might entail considerable time away from home.

Differences often arose between nomadic and settled communities. Nomads were attracted to the wealth of settled societies, so they redirected their movements accordingly, either for trading or raiding. Nomads and farmers often claimed the same land and water. Moreover, settled groups competed with their settled neighbors, which led to conflict and organized warfare.

Farming societies also needed to keep track of their material possessions and the duties and accomplishments of their people and deities. To do so, several settled societies around the world independently invented writing. These societies included the Sumerians and Egyptians (both circa 3500 to 3000 BCE); the Indus people (circa 2700 BCE); the Chinese (circa 1200 BCE); and the Mesoamericans (the Olmec circa 650 BCE and Zapotec circa 500 BCE). Administrators and priests recorded grain surpluses, taxes, services performed, the boundaries of the city and lands around it, their celebrated history, and their relations with the divine. In order to document the physical world around them, from the seventh century BCE onward, several cultures developed maps. Some of the earliest surviving human writing recounts migrations as well as tensions and exchanges with nomads or other settled communities.

Well-watered and fertile, Mesopotamia developed agriculture about 9000 BCE. By about 3500 BCE, people who spoke Sumerian began to concentrate in cities there. The earliest known such city is Uruk (by the lower Euphrates River in today's Iraq). Uruk's oral traditions were eventually written on clay tablets, some of which have survived until today. One such poem written about King Gilgamesh, who ruled sometime between 2750 and 2500 BCE, portrays him as a semi-divine being who brought culture and a protecting goddess to his city, subdued the surrounding nomads, and conquered widely, bringing back valuable resources. The poem reveals how Uruk's people regarded their world and the tensions between settled and nomadic ways of life.

Significantly, Gilgamesh's account begins and ends by celebrating his construction of the city's six-mile-long wall (its ruins have survived for 5,000 years). Addressing Uruk's proud people, the poem begins:

> Go up on the wall of Uruk and walk around,
> examine its foundation, inspect its brickwork thoroughly.
> Is not (even the core of) the brick structure made of kiln-fired brick. . . .[2]

Creating city walls required the assembled labor and skills of many people: leaders who designed and directed the construction as well as workers who shaped, fired, transported, and laid the bricks. Uruk's surviving tablets describe how Gilgamesh ordered young men to come build the wall, defend it, and participate in raids beyond it.

City walls served many critical purposes: controlling the entry and exit of animals and people; channeling drinking water and sewage; and marking off and defending the city's space from outsiders. Even small nomadic and settled communities learned to erect temporary fences against predatory animals and to enclose their domesticated animals. But settled communities often erected permanent barriers against nomadic herding communities who might regard crops and water as food and drink for themselves and their animals. Fixed walls thus defined the limits of formal control by the city's king and gods.

According to the tablets, Gilgamesh made each new bride in Uruk come to his palace and lie with him before she entered her husband's home. In most societies, a bride upon marriage customarily left her parents' household and migrated to the groom's household. Thus, people within the settled community migrated among households.

Cities also attracted or compelled immigration. Gilgamesh brought the goddess Ishtar and fixed her in a temple within the city, seeking to identify her protective power exclusively with Uruk. The tablets also recount how Gilgamesh tamed nomads and enticed them to the city, as represented by the character Enkidu:

> [Enkidu's] whole body was shaggy with hair. . . .
> He knew neither people nor settled living,
> but . . . ate grasses with the gazelles,
> and jostled at the watering hole with the animals;
> as with animals, his thirst was slaked with (mere) water.[3]

Gilgamesh used seduction by a city woman to make Enkidu "civilized," meaning a city dweller, wine-drinker, and Gilgamesh's subordinate. While Enkidu may not have formally been a slave, he served and obeyed Gilgamesh for the rest of his life. This pattern of incorporating—by recruitment, capture, or purchase—outsiders, often considered culturally inferior and alien, would continue as a distinctive kind of migration over the course of world history.

Cities have an insatiable need for raw materials and goods, as well as immigrants, both from the surrounding farms and from distant lands. Migrant traders and merchants arrive to barter or purchase products made by its artisans or wealth accumulated by its inhabitants. Further, cities mobilize armies to raid or wage war upon their neighbors. Gilgamesh, assisted by Enkidu (now representing Uruk's army), went on expeditions to seize resources, including cedar wood from distant mountain regions. They fought mountain communities that opposed his deforestation, timber confiscation, and seizure of land and water: "It was [Gilgamesh] who opened the mountain passes,/who dug wells on the flank of the mountain."[4] The story of Gilgamesh shows how the Sumerian people who had settled in Uruk oriented themselves to that place, developed new patterns of migration within and beyond their city wall, and dealt triumphantly with nomadic and other settled communities.

However, by 2350 BCE, a few hundred years after Gilgamesh's reign, the Sumerians of Uruk were overcome by a nomadic community of Akkadian-language speakers (another branch of the Semitic language family) from the Arabian peninsula, led by their warrior-king Sargon. The Akkadians then created their own empire, which subordinated several cities, among which the Akkadian rulers migrated. Indeed, much of human world history shows armed nomadic communities conquering settled societies and then settling themselves.

Due to cultural heritages or local environments, many people continued to live largely as migrants. Some regions, especially dryer ones, could not support farming (before mechanized irrigation). The vast grassy steppe that covers most of Eurasia, stretching 4,000 miles from the Great Hungarian Plain to western China, is too dry for trees or crops but is suitable for herding. Therefore, various herding communities on the Eurasian steppe mastered the potential of horses by selectively breeding, harnessing, riding, milking, and consuming them. From about 400 BCE, some steppe communities developed a powerful weapon especially suited to horsemen due to its short length: the powerful reflex bow composed from laminated layers of wood, horn, and sinew. The horse and bow made these nomads highly mobile hunters and warriors. Like nomads crossing Africa's Sahara or the North American Great Plains, they also provided raw materials, animal products, and surplus animals that were needed by settled farmers in exchange for grains and artisan-made goods including utensils, weapons, ornaments, and cloth.

From about 6000 BCE, the fertile soils watered by the Yellow and Yangtze rivers in China respectively enabled millet growing in the dryer, cooler north and wet rice in the warmer south. Using the accumulated wealth of farmers, artisans, and merchants, Chinese rulers built walled cities from about 3500 BCE. People increasingly migrated among them, either voluntarily as they sought new opportunities or forcibly as they were conscripted to build major state projects, including grand canals and standardized roads, which then fostered further migrations. The accumulated wealth of China also attracted trade and invasion by nomads.

Keeping predatory immigrants at bay was a major goal of each Chinese dynasty. The Qin (221–207 BCE) and then the Han (206 BCE–220 CE) sent thousands of workers and soldiers to construct and garrison the Great Wall across China's northern and western frontiers. Many Chinese then migrated to settle as farmers along it, forming both a cultural barrier against Central Asian nomads and also an economic link with them. Additionally, Chinese rulers used diplomacy to try to divide, buy off, or "civilize" steppe communities.

Occasionally, Han emperors sent cultured Chinese women to marry and Sinicize steppe chieftains. Hundreds of Chinese folksongs, stories, literary works, dramas, and films still celebrate one of these Han emigrant brides, the court beauty Wang Zhaojun. She was so beautiful that birds, seeing her, forgot to fly and fell to earth. In 33 BCE, she obeyed the Han emperor and reluctantly married a Xiongnu chief in order to pacify his steppe community. Yet, militant migrations from the steppe continued. Indeed, several major imperial dynasties in China began as invading nomads. Once having conquered, however, they settled as Chinese rulers and sought to keep other immigrants out. Even when steppe groups remained outside of China's land defenses, they affected its economy.

The major corridors of transcontinental trade that linked China, southern and western Asia, and Europe passed through the lands of nomadic communities who transported, raided, and also taxed this flow of precious goods. An elaborate fifth-century BCE burial of the extensively tattooed mummy of the "Ice Maiden" of the Pazyryk Valley in Siberia preserved her headdress, elaborate clothing, six sacrificed horses, and silver mirror. The riches in her grave suggest the wealth that nomadic cultures of the Eurasian steppe could accrue through herding, raiding, and especially trading. The most well known of these trading networks across Eurasia was later called the Silk Road (although it conveyed much more than silk).

Growing numbers of people also migrated for farming and trade into the fertile region surrounding the Nile River that ran north through Egypt to the Mediterranean. Diverse peoples had long walked along the banks of the Nile, floated down its current, or used oars and sails to voyage upstream. Increasingly, from around 6000 BCE, farmers planted crops on soil enriched by the Nile's seasonal flooding and irrigated from its water. Then, as kingdoms developed in the region from about 3500 BCE, merchants, generals, and officials collected crops, raw materials, crafts, and workers, both free and enslaved. By 3150 BCE, the kingdoms of the upper and lower Nile came together under the double-crown of the emperor, later called the pharaoh. This empire mobilized massive numbers for its armies, administration, and building projects, including irrigation works, cities, and pyramids. Successive imperial dynasties built and migrated through a series of capital cities. Their power extended beyond the Nile as merchants traveled long distances to trade in central Africa and west Asia.

The autobiographical inscription at Abydos of Weni the Elder (circa 2400 to 2250 BCE) describes migrations within and beyond Egypt. This imperial official was an immigrant from the upper to the lower Nile who then served the pharaoh in his court, as governor of several provinces, and as a conquering general of distant lands. Weni's epitaph boasts that the pharaoh assembled a vast and diverse army: "of many tens of thousands from all of Upper Egypt . . . from Lower Egypt . . . and from . . . Nubians."[5] Weni goes on to describe his own career as an enforcer of the pharaoh's law: "His majesty sent me at the head of this army . . . because of my rectitude, so that no one attacked his fellow, so that no one seized a loaf or sandals from a traveler, so that no one took a cloth from any town, so that no one took a goat from anyone." In addition to imposing the pharaoh's authority, Weni's army also destroyed Egypt's surrounding enemies:

> This army . . . had ravaged the Sand-dwellers' land. . . .
> It had cut down its figs, its vines. . . .
> It had slain its troops by many ten-thousands. . . .
> [It had carried] off many [troops] as captives. . . .
> His majesty praised me for it beyond anything. His majesty sent me
>     to lead this army five times. . . . I crossed in ships with these troops.

The pharaoh then commanded Weni to control Egypt's southern provinces and to bring raw materials northward: "my lord who lives forever, made me Count and Governor of Upper Egypt. . . . His majesty sent me to dig five canals in Upper Egypt, and to build three barges and four tow-boats of acacia wood. . . . Floated, they were loaded with very large granite blocks for the pyramid." A great diversity of people had immigrated into this Egyptian empire, either peacefully, or as war-captives or slaves, or as invaders.[6]

Around 1500 to 1200 BCE, Egyptians and other settled communities on the southern and eastern Mediterranean shores found strange (to them) "Sea People" suddenly arriving in ships, who raided the community and then sailed off again. Such predatory migrants proved elusive for the Egyptians to control or even identify. Like the Egyptians, scholars have not as yet determined the origins and identities of these nomadic Sea People. In a few instances, however, early accounts by nomads about their interactions with settled communities have survived.

By 8000 BCE on the steppe of west-central Asia, the Indo-European culture developed among cattle-herding nomadic communities. Like many other steppe peoples, their population periodically welled up and flowed outward, each branch fighting, trading, and mixing with each other and with the different local communities they encountered. The oral traditions of some Indo-European daughter cultures (written down much later) have preserved their values, their attitudes toward themselves and others, and their discoveries of the South Asian, Iranian, and European lands into which they variously migrated. About 1500 BCE, the Vedic-Sanskrit-speaking branch of this Indo-European culture migrated into India. There, they encountered settled communities who spoke various languages of the Dravidian linguistic family. These were the cultural and biological descendants of the once urbanized but by-then-dispersed Indus Valley civilization (circa 2700 to circa 1700 BCE).

Vedic-Sanskrit hymns celebrated the wheeled chariot–riding Indra as King of the Gods who defeated the local deity, Vrtra, who was worshipped by the farming peoples already settled there: "Indra took . . . the well-made golden thunderbolt with its thousand spikes . . . to do heroic deeds. He killed Vrtra and set free the flood of waters. . . . [Indra] the brave one . . . won the cows . . . [and] released the seven streams so that they could flow."[7] To nomadic herders, local farmers seemed to monopolize the water and land unjustly. They thus showed Indra rightly cutting down forests, splitting open mountains, liberating waters, capturing cattle, and seizing lands for his own worshippers. By about 500 BCE, these Vedic-Sanskrit-speaking immigrants themselves had largely settled in north India, adopting the farming systems of the worshippers of Vrtra and incorporating them into the lower ranks of Hindu society.

Other daughter branches of Indo-European culture migrated into Iran and Europe and settled there. Around 550 BCE, Cyrus the Great led his branch to conquer Persia (today's Iran) and establish the Achaemenid Empire. Other Indo-European groups settled across Europe, mixing biologically and culturally with local communities (linguists identify the Basque, Finnish, and Hungarian languages as stemming from these earlier non-Indo-European cultures). Much later, from the sixteenth century onward, European colonizers moved out across much of the globe and imposed their Indo-European languages on other communities. Today, three billion people, almost half of all humans, speak one or more of the 140 current Indo-European languages.

During the period circa 1050 to circa 600 BCE, Greek-language speakers gradually scattered like seeds across the islands and lands of the eastern Mediterranean and west Asia, describing this process as *diaspora*, meaning "sowed or dispersed over." After a community begins to identify strongly with a geographical region as its sacred homeland, it experiences a collective sense of loss and a hope of future return when forced to emigrate. Even if people voluntarily emigrate, they may still continue to identify strongly with the land they left behind. "Diaspora" customarily also describes scattered members of the Jewish community following the destruction of their Temple in Jerusalem by the Babylonian army in 586 BCE and then again following a major wave of dispersion from their Holy Land after their defeat by the Romans in 70 CE. Armenians now also use the word "diaspora" to describe their forced dispersion during the reign of the Byzantine emperor Maurice (539–602 CE) to Bulgaria and again after World War I across Europe and the Americas. Many people refer to the African diaspora of enslaved emigrants across the Atlantic and Indian Oceans from the sixteenth through the nineteenth

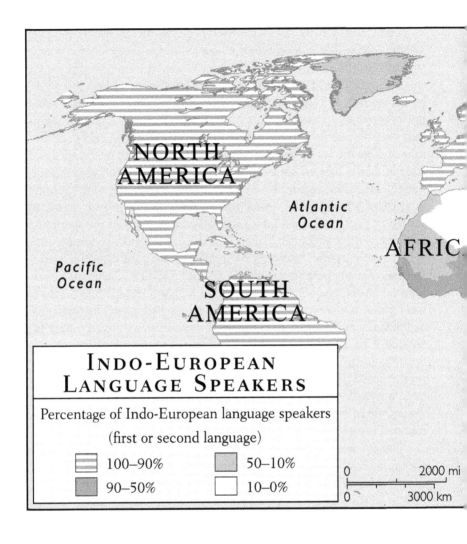

## INDO-EUROPEAN LANGUAGE SPEAKERS

Percentage of Indo-European language speakers
(first or second language)

100–90%    50–10%
90–50%     10–0%

0          2000 mi
0          3000 km

centuries. Irish, Chinese, Indians, and other communities have also now used diaspora to identify their (often coerced) time away from their remembered, but long distant, homelands. However, once diaspora networks have been established, they can provide support for trade, future immigrants, and even future conquerors.

Emperor Alexander (r. 336–323 BCE), who inherited the throne of Macedonia at age twenty, soon determined to conquer the world; he began by subjugating the Balkans and Greece. In 334 BCE, while still a prince, he left his home, never to return. A Greek historian, Diodorus, recalled that, as Alexander first landed in Asia, "he flung his spear from

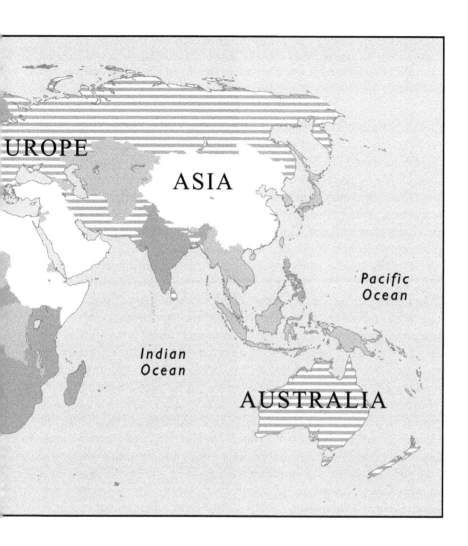

the ship and fixed it in the ground, and then leapt ashore himself, the first of the Macedonians, signifying that he received Asia from the gods as a spear-won prize."[8] Alexander then led his soldiers across Anatolia, the eastern Mediterranean, Egypt, and the Persian Achaemenid Empire. Among the many diverse communities his armies encountered were from the earlier Greek diaspora. By 327 BCE, Alexander had led his army into India. But there:

> Alexander observed that his soldiers were exhausted with their constant campaigns. They had spent almost eight years among toils and dangers. . . . There had been many losses among the soldiers, and

no relief from fighting was in sight. The hooves of the horses had been worn thin by steady marching. The arms and armour were wearing out, and Greek clothing was quite gone. They had to clothe themselves in foreign materials, recutting the garments of the Indians.[9]

Although Alexander wanted to continue east to the end of the world, his soldiers convinced him to return westward. After a decade of campaigning, he died in Babylon at age thirty-two. His army's martial migrations left behind distant colonies (including many cities named after Alexander) with amalgamated Greek and local cultures, biological descendants, and newly opened intercontinental trade routes that linked Greece, Egypt, and India, along which many subsequent ideas, goods, and people would travel for centuries thereafter.

Buddhism took a more peaceful path of expansion across Asia. During the sixth to fifth centuries BCE in South Asia, Gautama the Buddha, the "enlightened one," taught nonviolence and social status based on personal achievement rather than on ancestry. Both these values appealed to Indian merchants who had gained wealth but still held relatively low status in the Hindu social order, which was determined by birth. Buddhism also advocated renunciation of home and possessions for monks and nuns, who migrated seasonally as religious mendicants.

Emperor Ashoka Maurya (r. 268–232 BCE), after conquering most of north India, proclaimed his conversion to Buddhism. He then enforced its ideals of peacefully following the "Middle Path" of righteousness. Ashoka had Buddhist edicts carved into rocks guarding the borders of his empire and notifying immigrants that they were entering a land under Buddhist authority. He and his successors also supported migrating teachers and missionaries to spread Buddhism throughout Asia.

Eventually, Buddhist missionaries made converts across Sri Lanka and Southeast Asia as well as across Afghanistan and into China, Korea, and Japan. In each region, the local population adapted Buddhism to fit its indigenous culture. Pilgrims, such as the early fifth-century CE Chinese Buddhist monk Faxian, traveled through Central Asia, Nepal, India, and Sri Lanka to acquire the Buddha's original teachings. Many cultures revere their own sacred migrations but some seek to control the migrations of others.

Romans traced their own origins to the divinely guided immigration of Aeneas and his family, refugees from Troy (in today's Turkey) after its defeat by invading Greeks. Indeed, the Roman Republic (509 to 49 BCE) and then Empire (in Rome until 330 CE) celebrated migrations, but also used and feared migrants. As Roman power grew, conquering much of

Europe, north Africa, and west Asia, it attracted ever more diverse immigrants. In the first century CE, an immigrant to Rome, Iberian-born poet Martial, rhetorically addressed his emperor, celebrating the diversity of the imperial capital:

> What race is so distant from us, what race is so barbarous, O Caesar, that from it no spectator is present in your city! The cultivator of Rhodope [in Thrace] is here from Haemus, sacred to Orpheus. The Scythian [from Central Asia] who drinks the blood of his horses is here; he, too, who quaffs the waters of the Nile nearest their springing [in Sudan]; and he also whose shore is laved by the most distant ocean. The Arabian has hastened hither; the Sabaeans have hastened [from Yemen]; and here the Cilicians [from southern Anatolia] have anointed themselves with their own native perfume. Here come the Sicambrians [from north-central Europe] with their hair all twisted into a knot, and here the frizzled Ethiopians. Yet though their speech is all so different, they all speak together hailing you, O Emperor, as the true father of your country.[10]

Martial thus portrayed the diverse exotic subjects from the empire's distant boundaries who came to Rome to revere the emperor.

In addition to attracting immigrants to their imperial capital, Romans also forcibly moved people around their empire. Roman society depended heavily on about ten million slaves. Since Roman citizens could not be legally enslaved, they imported individuals and groups captured or purchased from marginal European, Asian, and African communities. The Roman term for slave is derived from Slav, a major source of its slaves.

Slavs followed a farming-based culture along and beyond the Roman Empire's northeastern frontier. Their culture contained a whole family of languages and biologically diverse peoples. Some had recently immigrated from Central Asia into eastern Europe; others had lived in Europe for generations. But all adopted Slavic languages and farming technologies, which Romans considered crude and uncivilized.

The Roman state systematically sought to manage immigration by nomadic communities that pressed against its borders seeking trading or raiding access to Rome's wealth. Roman armies drove subject communities from one borderland to another or beyond the imperial frontier. Romans often tried to settle one tribe in a strategic location to block incursions by others.

A Roman network of walls, ditches, garrisons, forts, and river defenses, all linked by military roads, stretched across its European northern boundary, from the Black Sea along the Danube and Rhine rivers. The westernmost section was Hadrian's Wall along the northern border of his province of Britain. The Roman state encouraged retired soldiers to move to colonies along these frontier defenses as a further barrier against the barbarians beyond. Veterans who served twenty years received grants of land there for farming or mining. Often, they married local women, resulting in communities with mixed heritage, but, because citizenship legally followed the father's line, children of these unions were Roman citizens. The farming and mining was mainly done by imported or local slaves. Empires valued walls and boundary controls, but nomadic communities constantly challenged them.

From about 250 CE onward, pressure on the Roman imperial frontiers increased, especially from various Germanic and other steppe communities. In 380 CE, the historian Ammianus Marcellinus, who spent much of his life defending Rome's embattled frontiers, dismissively described the constant migratory way of life of alien Germanic communities:

> [Germans] never shelter themselves under roofed houses . . . but they wander about, roaming over the mountains and the woods . . . [and] they never enter a house unless under the compulsion of some extreme necessity. . . . They have no settled abode, but are homeless and lawless, perpetually wandering with their wagons, which they make their homes; in fact they seem to be people always in flight. Their wives live in these wagons, and there weave their miserable garments; and here too they sleep with their husbands, and bring up their children till they reach the age of puberty; nor, if asked, can any one of them tell you where he was born, as he was conceived in one place, born in another at a great distance, and brought up in another still more remote.[11]

Marcellinus further denigrated Germans as inferior to Romans for lacking an established political system and settled farming: "They are not under the authority of a king, but are contented with the irregular government of their nobles. . . . None of them plough, or even touch a plough-handle." But, he had to admit, "they force their way through all obstacles," including through the Roman Empire's fortified boundaries. Although Marcellinus was not ethnographically accurate about the constant nomadic life of all Germanic communities, his view reflected the apprehensive stereotypes of Roman elites about these migrants, many coming from central and west Asia, speaking not Latin but rather other Indo-European languages.

Under pressure from nomadic peoples, Emperor Constantine (r. 306–337 CE) believed Rome indefensible and moved his imperial capital to Constantinople in 330. Constantine understood the danger of immigrating peoples, having before his enthronement traveled through much of the Roman Empire, including Britain and elsewhere on imperial frontiers. Constantine also sought to strengthen his authority by linking his rule with Christianity, a rising religion that had for three centuries been spreading through missionaries, pilgrims, and persecuted but faithful communities.

Constantine's fears proved justified, as when nomadic Goths sacked Rome in 410. Goths included a coalition of various Germanic peoples who joined together for predatory migrations into the lands of settled communities. Similarly, other nomadic cultures coalesced to become the Vandals, who migrated thousands of miles across the northern Roman Empire and Spain, and then established a kingdom in North Africa (today Tunisia) in 429. In 455, Vandals crossed the Mediterranean to sack Rome.

Such predatory migrations were most powerful when mobilized by a charismatic leader who brought diverse people together to form an awe-inspiring *horde* (originally meaning in many Central Asian languages, "royal encampment"). One such leader, Attila the Hun (r. 434–453), inspired a powerful multiethnic alliance that ravaged the western Roman Empire. Nomadic communities moving out from the population pump of Central Asia formed the bulk of his followers. Hun steppe communities had technological advantages such as unmatched light cavalry, who were armed with powerful composite reflex bows and long sabers. Various emigrating branches of the Hun pressed against surrounding settled empires, including China, which evidently called these people the Xiongnu and struggled to defend the Great Wall against them. The rulers of India and Iran likewise fought militant Hun immigrants. But after Attila's death, his fragile coalition in Europe fragmented. The cultural impact of these predatory migrations persist; their names still seem threatening in English today: Goths, Vandals, horde, Attila, Huns.

Yet, by the sixth century in Europe, many of these formerly migratory communities had settled and mixed with the substantial local populations. Over time, many of these amalgamated ethnicities bonded with their lands and would become the current European nationalities, including Franks and Burgundians in today's France, Lombards in northern Italy, Angles and Saxons in England, and Slavs in eastern Europe. Elsewhere in the world, other patterns of migration were developing, shaped by local environments.

Each of sub-Saharan Africa's many ecologically and culturally defined regions also had its own migration history. Expanding trans-Saharan trade, especially based on camel caravans, enhanced the export northward of gold as well as slaves, cloth, and other goods in exchange for salt and other products. Enriched by this trade, a series of cities and regional states formed along the Niger River in west Africa.

In some areas of sub-Saharan Africa, endemic diseases limited the use of cattle and other draft animals. But the spreading use of metals for iron axes and other implements enabled a growing number of people to clear forests and extend their farmlands. The different branches of communities speaking a language in the Bantu family gradually spread out from west Africa (from circa 1500 BCE) over much of central and southern Africa, mixing with local communities to produce the 400 to 500 distinct cultures there today.

During the long period between about 100,000 BCE and 600 CE, which includes about 90 percent of our history as Homo sapiens, almost all of our genetic changes occurred. The total human population was minuscule compared with what it is today. Hence, as groups of humans expanded within Africa and also into previously uninhabited regions of the earth, many communities moved into relative isolation from each other across the globe.

Each local community developed a distinct culture, including language, and gradually adapted to its specific environment through genetic mutations that led to natural selection. Each region's environment favored particular physical characteristics—like the ability to function in the presence of a disease or with more or less sunlight. For example, the high plateau of Tibet, 2.8 miles above sea level, favored people with a genetic mutation that enables tolerance of the lower oxygen levels there. Hence, people with chance or environmentally caused genetic mutations that proved advantageous thrived and reproduced more effectively in that particular environment.

Gradually, visually distinct characteristics, like color of eyes, hair, or skin, came to predominate in certain regions due both to these adaptive mutations as well as to "genetic drift," that is, the random preservation of genetic variations that sometimes occurs in isolated populations, even if these variations have no particular adaptive advantage. Communities that moved into certain ecological regions developed similar phenotypes—outward appearance, or what are commonly called "breeds" in animals and (although not accurate in biological terms) are called in humans, "races." Most visible, or phenotype, variation occurs along gradients. The amount of direct sunlight (ultraviolet rays) decreases as one moves north or south of the earth's equatorial zone; this is reflected in the decreased amount of pigmentation (melanin) in the skin of local human communities. But similar phenotypes often contain different genotypes, or genetic composition. The basic genotype of all humans makes us a single species, however apparently different a few features of our regionally based phenotypes may be.

Over centuries, as local populations diversified culturally and physiologically, many began to think of themselves as different from other Homo sapiens. But, as people have continued to migrate and intermarry with people from different regions, many of these earlier genetic distinctions have mixed; further, communities have divided, merged, and developed new cultural blends. Hence, almost all people today have biological and cultural heritages from various parts of the world, although one descent line may appear to be predominant.

By 600 CE, Homo sapiens had migrated by land and by water across all the earth (excepting only Antarctica and some isolated islands). Our human species adapted to the variety of environments it encountered and also developed new technologies of production, transportation, and communication that enhanced its abilities to move people and their possessions. Our global population rose to about 300 million, but this was relatively small (less than the current population of the United States alone). Many people would continue to live as nomads but a growing proportion would settle in the earth's more fertile regions and develop new migration patterns there. Militant migrating communities occupied new lands and drove out or mixed with the local people. Settled communities also formed states that tried to control the movements of others, especially by excluding immigrants they considered different from themselves.

CHAPTER 2

# Mixing and Clashing Migrations, 600 to 1450 CE

"And those who emigrated for [the cause of] Allah after they had been wronged—We will surely settle them in this world in a good place; but the reward of the Hereafter is greater, if only they could know."[1] The fifty-two-year-old Prophet Muhammad recited this divine Quranic promise that he heard from Archangel Gabriel soon before he and his early followers emigrated in 622 from his hostile hometown of Mecca. There, he, his family, and other fellow Muslims had endured persecution for following Islam, including its monotheistic faith in Allah. The Prophet and his faithful companions moved two hundred miles to Medina where the people welcomed them and formed the first Muslim community. For many Muslims, the Prophet Muhammad and his early companions continue to represent moral ideals. This first emigration for the sake of Islam, the *Hijra*, starts the Islamic *Hijri* calendar and has continued as a religious model for Muslims ever since.

For fourteen centuries becoming a *Muhajir*, one who migrates for the sake of Islam, has remained a powerful concept. About six million people who immigrated to the new Muslim nation of Pakistan at its creation in 1947 are still called Muhajirs, along with their descendants born within Pakistan. They take pride in their status as immigrants for the sake of Islam, but many indigenous Muslim regional ethnicities in the lands that became Pakistan regard them as outsiders who had come as refugees and then assumed undue leadership over their adopted nation.

In 1324, Mansa Musa, king of Mali, traveled 3,500 miles overland across the Sahara and north Africa on *Hajj*, the pilgrimage to Mecca during the holy lunar month. He brought vast wealth in gold that his kingdom had mined and accumulated through trade. An Arab historian, al-Umari, who had himself emigrated from Damascus to Cairo, recalled:

[Mansa Musa] flooded Cairo with his benefactions. He left no court emir nor holder of a royal office without the gift of a load of gold. The Cairenes made incalculable profits out of him and his suite in buying and selling and giving and taking. They exchanged gold until they depressed its value in Egypt and caused its price to fall.[2]

Islam requires all Muslims to make at least one Hajj, if they are able. Today, about three million pilgrims from throughout the multicontinental Islamic world annually complete the Hajj, earning the honorific *Hajji*.

Mansa Musa, like all Hajjis, powerfully experienced in Mecca the global array of Muslim men and women who assembled as one Islamic community: speaking many different languages, embodying nearly all human physical features, but all dressed identically as Hajjis and simultaneously performing the same rituals. In many lands, Muslims also migrate on "lesser" pilgrimages to the graves of the Prophet Muhammad's descendants and of other spiritually powerful Muslims.

*Each year during the lunar month of* Hajj *("Pilgrimage"), millions of Muslims journey from around the world to Mecca to perform elaborate rituals culminating in their final circumambulation of the* Ka'aba, *a cubical stone building covered in black cloth decorated with gold embroidery. Historically, some Muslims have settled in Mecca, but most travel home bearing the honorific* Hajji. Photo courtesy Omar Chatriwala of Al Jazeera English

Historically, the Arabian peninsula's dry environment has supported little settled agriculture and many nomadic trading, herding, and raiding Arab tribal communities, including Jews and Christians, speaking various Semitic languages. Arabia also had commercial towns on inland and shoreline trade routes that profited from its strategic location—southeast of the Byzantine Empire based in Constantinople, southwest of the Sassanian Empire of Iran, east of Egypt, and linked by the seasonal monsoon winds to eastern Africa and Asia. The Prophet Muhammad had himself traveled widely as a long-distance merchant. But Arabia's location also meant the surrounding empires preyed upon it, until the emergence of the dynamically expansive Islamic community.

During the lifetime of the Prophet Muhammad and within the century following his death, Muslim merchants, Sufis, scholars, and rulers migrated long distances and converted many people of the local Eurasian and African communities with whom they interacted. Dar al-Islam, "the Land of Islam," rapidly expanded outward: across the Levant into Anatolia, forcing back the Byzantine Eastern Roman Empire; across

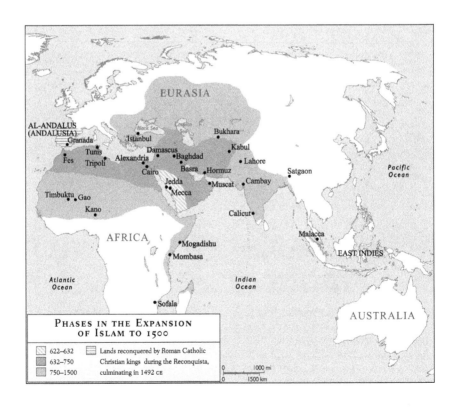

PHASES IN THE EXPANSION
OF ISLAM TO 1500

622–632
632–750
750–1500

Lands reconquered by Roman Catholic
Christian kings during the Reconquista,
culminating in 1492 CE

0          1000 mi
0       1500 km

Iran, defeating the Sassanian Empire; across north Africa and into Iberia and southern France; along the east African coast; and into Asia. Although Iberia was gradually reconquered by Roman Catholic Christian kings from the eighth to fifteenth centuries, the Islamic community continued to extend outward through migration and conversion.

These dramatic and extensive expansions created the vision of a unified Muslim global community, *umma*, within which all Muslims were equals and could migrate freely. Significantly, a decreasing proportion of Muslims were Arabs. Rather, diverse local nomadic and settled communities accepted Islam, convinced that conversion brought not only salvation but also worldly success. Each community then adapted many Muslim social practices in light of its own distinctive culture.

The historian and philosopher, Ibn Khaldun, migrated over his tumultuous lifetime during the fourteenth century from his birthplace in Tunis, to Morocco, Islamic Spain, and then as far east as Damascus, Syria. He insightfully noted:

> When the conditions of the inhabitants of the desert reach the utmost ease and become most profitable, they look for tranquility and quiet. Therefore, they settle in towns and cities. . . . Whenever people settle . . . and amass luxuries and become accustomed to a life of abundance and refinement, their bravery decreases to the degree that their wildness and desert habits decrease.[3]

Ibn Khaldun himself grew up among the Berbers, a fierce nomadic community. But, as they prospered, they settled and migrated to cities for a more contented lifestyle. He lived his last years among the urbane Arabs of Cairo.

Dar al-Islam created a multicontinental arena within which many diverse Muslims and non-Muslims had the opportunity and motivation to migrate long distances. The prominent Abbasid dynasty of Sunni Caliphs in Baghdad (750–1258) established a uniform system of law, administration, coinage, and communication that assisted merchants trading on sea or land throughout much of Asia and north Africa. Muslims, and trade diaspora communities including Jews, Christians, and Hindus, could obtain information about distant markets and uniform justice almost everywhere they traveled under Abbasid authority or influence.

By 1450, many of the globe's most extensive transcontinental trade networks had become predominantly Muslim. As the merchants, caravan drivers, and sailors who conducted this commerce gradually accepted

*Many nomadic communities have long carried trade goods as well as Islamic culture and sciences south across the Sahara desert; they have also carried northward goods and ideas produced in sub-Saharan Africa. Tuareg Berbers continue to migrate, including this woman and boy photographed in southern Algeria in 2004.* Photo courtesy Garrondo

Islam, so too did many local traders, intermediaries, and rulers among whom they moved. One intercontinental trading network around the Mediterranean linked Morocco, the Sahel (the southern "shore" of the Sahara desert), southern Europe, Egypt, and Arabia. The Silk Road connected the eastern Mediterranean, Iran, Afghanistan, India, and China. Yet another network, on ships powered by monsoon winds, joined Arabia, the coasts of the Indian Ocean, and the western Pacific. In each region, distinctive Muslim-centered cultures evolved out of diverse origins; along the east African coast, Africans, Arabs, Persians, and Indians developed a common trading language: Swahili.

Islamic scholars, *ulema*, also migrated throughout Dar al-Islam and beyond; students traveled widely to study with them. They disseminated Arabic language and culture, especially the holy Quran, accounts of the words and deeds of the Prophet Mohammad, known as *Hadith*, and the expanding Islamic sciences including medicine, astronomy, and engineering. Learned Muslim travelers also incorporated new ideas and discoveries from the local communities among whom they moved. Notably, Arab mathematicians collected, systematized, and advanced Greek, Persian, and Indian knowledge, which they called *al-jebra* (now algebra in English). Conversely, local people throughout the Islamic world gained literacy in Arabic so they could participate in this vast and growing shared knowledge.

From early on in Islam, many Muslims sought a deeply personal relationship with Allah. Various Muslim holy men and women, known as Sufis, developed ways to reach this mystical experience through using devotional, meditative, or ecstatic techniques. Their followers, many of whom became masters themselves, formed devotional traditions that spread their specific Sufi practices ever farther. In Asia, vast numbers of devotees assemble annually at the graves of Sufis on their death anniversary, when they migrated to heaven through an *urs*, or "wedding," with Allah. As Sufi religious orders developed and extended throughout the Islamic world and beyond its frontiers, they conveyed not only their mystical religious traditions but often also technology.

Sufis from western Asia who immigrated to the arid but potentially fertile lands of Central Asia, western China, and northwest India brought inspirational Islamic practices. They also brought water-lifting and channeling technologies, including the Persian waterwheel, with its continuous circle of buckets conveying underground water to the surface. These technologies enabled nomadic herders to settle by irrigating lands hitherto too dry for farming. Other Sufis brought to densely forested eastern India and Southeast Asia metal ax and heavy plow technologies that enabled forest people to clear farmland and settle. As local herders and forest dwellers became farmers, their populations rose, they became more prosperous, and they accepted the eclectic Islam taught by these Muslim holy men. Similarly, Sufis landing on the coasts of India and Southeast Asia incorporated local merchants and artisans into transoceanic commercial networks, simultaneously converting them to Islam. Some of the world's largest and densest Muslim populations today result from such Sufi immigrants and teachers.

Muslims also developed military and political sciences that enabled leaders of nomadic communities to found and administer expansive states and also empowered rulers of settled kingdoms to extend them. The *greater jihad* is the inner holy struggle by individuals to become good Muslims, but the *lesser jihad* is the outer holy struggle to protect and spread Islam. Some Muslim warlords used the lesser jihad to motivate their followers to conquer non-Muslims or Muslims following a different branch of Islam. Some Muslim rulers forced their non-Muslim subjects to convert, to pay a special tax called *jizya*, or else to migrate away. Many local people accepted Islam willingly or perforce due to Muslim rulers. Muslim kingdoms across Central, South, and Southeast Asia also developed sophisticated bureaucratic systems, some derived from the pre-Islamic Sassanian Empire, which proved particularly effective.

Steppe nomads of Central Asia, often Turkic-language speakers, at various times conquered the surrounding lands. Usually they then at least partially adopted the culture of their new subjects. As Turks settled as rulers in China, they Sinicized as the Sui dynasty (581–618). In western Asia, they became Muslims. One branch, the Seljuk Turks, seized Baghdad in 1055, in 1453 captured Constantinople (renamed Istanbul in the nineteenth century), and created the Ottoman Empire, which lasted until 1923.

Historically, Muslims have imported many different types of slaves into Dar al-Islam. In the Quran (although not always in practice), Muslim men and women should not be enslaved while non-Muslims can be. But slaves have various legal rights and protections while serving their Muslim owners. For example, a slave who has a child with her Muslim master is freed, along with their children.

Slaves emigrated unwillingly into Dar al-Islam from central Africa northward across the Sahara, from east Africa across the Indian Ocean into Arabia and South Asia, and from eastern Europe into the Ottoman Empire. Many slaves had been captured in war or sold by their families. Some Muslim owners converted their slaves to Islam, but others deliberately kept them as non-Muslims so that they remained alien from the surrounding Muslim society, and therefore dependent on their master.

A few enslaved immigrants rose to power and prominence in Muslim society. Slave wives or consorts of powerful Muslim men might gain significant influence in their households, especially if they gave birth to the male heir. Male slaves also occasionally rose to high office. In many societies, powerful patriarchs customarily used their sons as administrators of their kingdom or family business. But a father could only have a limited number of biological sons, and few of these could be trusted fully not to challenge or depose their father. Hence, some patriarchs trained domestic slaves as surrogate sons.

"One obedient slave is better than three hundred sons; for the latter desire their father's death, the former his master's glory," observed Nizam al-Mulk, an eleventh-century Persian scholar and powerful official in the Seljuk Turkish kingdom.[4] Because a slave usually could not displace his master or inherit rule or property, he was believed less dangerous than a son. The practice of using large numbers of imported military slaves expanded under the Abbasid Caliphate, and many rulers subsequently deployed such troops along their frontiers where their hereditary rule was less stable and established. Yet, some particularly charismatic slaves established their own kingdoms. The first ruling "Slave" dynasty (1206–90) of India's Delhi Sultanate were Turks who had been captured and enslaved in Afghanistan, sent out by their royal master to conquer and govern north India, but who then gained their independence. Dar al-Islam thus included a diversity of settled and migrant communities and cultures in large parts of Eurasia and Africa.

"It was a habit of mine on my travels never, so far as possible, to retrace any road that I had once travelled over. . . . I have indeed—praise be to God—attained my desire in this world, which was to travel through the earth, and I have attained in this respect what no other person has attained."[5] So said Ibn Battuta, a fourteenth-century north African Berber Muslim scholar, who traveled for thirty years, motivated both by his religious faith and also by his desire to explore Dar al-Islam. He set out at age twenty-one from his Moroccan homeland on Hajj to Arabia, then journeyed along the east African coast, across Iran and South and Southeast Asia to China, with other excursions through Iberia and west Africa. He claimed to have walked, ridden camels and horses, and sailed 75,000 miles. Wherever he immigrated, he found Muslims who appreciated his scholarship in Islamic sciences, his Arabic culture, and particularly his expertise in Islamic law. Everywhere, he met many other travelers.

While in Calicut (today called Kozhikode), south India, Ibn Battuta encountered ships from China, unfamiliar to him in rigging, construction, and private luxury: "The Chinese vessels [called] junks . . . have sails, which are made of bamboo rods plaited into mats. They are never lowered, but turned according to the direction of the wind; at anchor they are left floating in the wind. . . . The vessel has four decks and contains rooms, cabins, and saloons for merchants; a cabin has chambers and a lavatory, and can be locked by its occupants."[6] Indeed, many Chinese had long been emigrating and trading throughout Southeast Asia and the Indian Ocean.

Zheng He, a Muslim eunuch, described his epic fifteenth-century voyages: "We have traversed more than [30,000 miles] of immense water spaces and have beheld in the ocean huge waves like mountains rising in the sky, and we have set eyes on barbarian regions far away . . . , while our sails, loftily unfurled like clouds day and night, continued their course . . . , traversing those savage waves as if we were treading a public thoroughfare."[7]

The first Chinese Ming emperor had entrusted command of seven successive armadas, called "Treasure Fleets," to Zheng He. He descended from a Persian official who had migrated to Yunnan, south China. At age eleven, he was captured by the Ming army, castrated but not enslaved, and then entrusted with ever greater administrative responsibilities. From 1405 to 1433, he led a series of maritime expeditions, each consisting of several hundred ships and thousands of men. Sophisticated Chinese shipbuilding and navigation technologies such as the compass and cartography enabled these vast fleets of huge ships to sail beyond maritime Southeast Asia as far as India, Arabia, and east Africa.

Throughout his voyages, Zheng He gathered information, specimen animals, and artifacts from those distant lands. He exchanged diplomatic gifts with diverse rulers, symbolically incorporating them into the Chinese tribute system centered on the Ming emperor, ruler of the Middle Kingdom with the Mandate of Heaven. In Southeast Asia, he left colonies of Chinese men behind; he also discovered scattered colonies of Chinese who had earlier emigrated overseas. Most Chinese colonizers were men, so they married local women to form mixed cultures. But the Ming dynasty (1368–1644) then turned its attention inland, repudiating oceanic expeditions (even destroying records of Zheng He's voyages), and outlawing further Chinese overseas emigration. Indeed, many rulers have attempted to control migration and their frontiers.

Over the centuries, various groups had immigrated and settled across the Japanese islands, especially in ecological regions suitable for highly productive wet-rice agriculture. Buddhism and other cultural influences entered through missionaries and other travelers from China. According to Japanese tradition, the imperial dynasty (still on the throne today) descended from heaven (although many scholars assert they immigrated to Japan from Korea). On earth, this dynasty first settled in their capital of Nara (710 to 794), then migrated to Kyoto (994 to 1869), and then to Tokyo (1869 to present).

The Japanese imperial state regulated migration within the Japanese islands. Peasants were largely bound to the land and people who did not have a local identity often appeared suspicious. Although merchants might be wealthier, as people who depended on trade, they had lesser status than samurai warriors or even settled peasants. The Japanese imperial system incorporated regionally based clan leaders, called *daimyo*, who provided to the emperor military service by their samurai followers and also land revenues from their estates. Daimyo were also personally attracted to the prestigious imperial court.

"I was brought up in a distant province [Kazusa, today Chiba prefecture] which lies farther than the farthest end of the Eastern Road. I am ashamed to think that inhabitants of the Royal City will think me an uncultured girl."[8] Lady Sarashina recounted these emotions in her personal diary, written from 1009 to 1059, about what it was like as a youth to leave her provincial home, where her father had been sent as governor, and migrate about three hundred miles to the awe-inspiring imperial court at Kyoto. Like her, many emigrants from rural to urban environments (and also youths entering a university or new career) feel apprehensive about how they will measure up. She later described moving to serve in an imperial household: "I went to the Princess's apartments every night and lay down among unknown persons, so I could not sleep at all. I was bashful and timid and wept in secret . . . longing for home where my old and weak parents, making much of me, relied upon me as if I were worthy of it. I yearned for them and felt very lonely. Unfortunate, deplorable, and helpless mind!"[9] Most people experience personal migration between households as they grow up. Anxiety and homesickness due to leaving one's home were intensified in her case by the overwhelming preeminence of the imperial family.

The empire eventually conquered all the people of the Japanese archipelago. Although the Japanese imperial dynasty remained on the throne, its control declined from the tenth century onward. Instead, many regionally based daimyo competed for power. The generalissimo who subdued and largely incorporated the most resistant marginal communities, including the Jomon people in the north of the main Honshu Island, gained the title Shogun, "Defeater of Barbarians." From the late twelfth century onward, shoguns appropriated power from the imperial dynasty, which retained its sovereignty in ritual only. Expansive migrating communities, using new cultures and technologies, were simultaneously expanding across the world.

Scandinavians, during the eighth to twelfth centuries, created their distinctive longship and the culture of "going Viking" that energized their far-reaching migrations across Eurasia and to North America. They developed these innovative vessels by fastening a mast with a yardarm and square sail into their narrow, shallow-draft, rowing craft. These light but sturdy vessels had little internal framing. Instead Scandinavians cut long thin boards from the tall, close-grained trees of their forests, overlapped each plank, and fastened them using iron nails. Rowing benches gave further strength to the hull; larger longships had thirty-five benches (one longship unearthed in Ireland had fifty benches).

These longships had the flexibility to ride over swells and, to pierce waves, they had raised bows and sterns, which were often decorated with dragon heads and tails. In calm waters, their low bulwarks meant lighter vessels. But in storms or battle, crews could mount their shields along the longship's sides for protection, raising them against oncoming waves or arrows. Not having keels, these boats could be hauled ashore or portaged but could not sail as well to windward and were vulnerable to violent Atlantic storms. Riding low in the water, with no decks and only an erectable cloth tent for shelter, the fastest of these craft, used for raiding, could carry only limited passengers, cargo, a few animals, and precious goods like gold and silver. Broader but slower versions of these Scandinavian longships could carry more cargo and passengers and were used to conduct overseas trade or establish trans-Atlantic colonies.

The old Norse Eddas (oral traditions of historical narrative later written down) celebrated ambitious and entrepreneurial heroes who

*In 1893, a dozen Norwegians under Captain Magnus Andersen sailed an eighty-foot longship from Norway across the Atlantic to Newfoundland in four weeks and then via New York to Lake Michigan for Chicago's Columbian Exposition. Andersen's vessel was the replica of a longship unearthed at Gokstad, Norway, after having been buried since 900 CE.* Photo by Edward H. Hart, courtesy Library of Congress, Prints and Photographs Division, LC-D4-21183 ventured on longships into foreign lands. Scandinavians participated in commerce across Europe and also preyed upon it. Seeking opportunities and profit not available in their homeland, they migrated west across the north Atlantic and south to the Mediterranean, both along Europe's west coast and down the north-south flowing rivers of western Russia. The wealth and adventurous accounts they brought back enthused other men and emigrant families to travel to distant lands. The arrival of a Scandinavian Great Army, however, often meant disaster for the local population.

A French eyewitness bewailed a Norse assault on Paris in 885, the last of four such invasions during the ninth century alone: "The Northmen came to Paris, with 700 sailing ships, not counting those of smaller size. . . . At one stretch the Seine [River] was lined with the vessels for more than [six miles], so that one might ask in astonishment in what cavern the river had been swallowed up, since it was not to be seen."[10] After much fighting around Paris, Carolingian emperor Charles the Fat (r. 881–888) "allowed the Northmen to have the country of Sens to plunder; and in the spring he gave them 700 pounds of silver on condition that by the month of March they leave France for their own kingdom."[11] Then Emperor Charles, hoping to prevent further raids by other Scandinavians, convinced one Norse leader, Rolf, to settle with his followers as Charles's feudal subordinate in the region of northwestern France henceforth named Normandy after the Norsemen. Rolf was baptized Robert when he and many of his followers converted to Roman Catholicism and intermarried with the local population.

Scandinavians had also immigrated into much of Scotland, northern and eastern England, and Ireland raiding as well as settling as farmers and marrying local women. Danish immigrants conquered the Danelaw region in north-central England. In addition, Scandinavian men and their wives—many of them Scottish or Irish—then migrated to uninhabited northern Atlantic islands, including Iceland (from around 900 CE). Consequently, 62 percent of Icelanders today have mtDNA from their Scottish or Irish maternal ancestry but 75 percent of male Icelanders have Y-chromosomes from their Scandinavian paternal lineage.[12] Icelanders and other Scandinavian emigrants then established colonies in Greenland for over 460 years, before abandoning them by 1450 as the global cooling of the Little Ice Age made farming unviable there.

Simultaneously, Scandinavians migrated south on the rivers of eastern Europe, down to the Black Sea, and then the Mediterranean. They traded and raided for furs, slaves, silver, and luxury goods from the Byzantine Empire, the Abbasid Caliphate, and the transcontinental Silk Road. During the previous centuries, Slavic cultures had been spreading across eastern Europe and assimilating local communities into their farming way of life and languages. The incoming Scandinavians, called Varangians, used their military and commercial prowess to conquer and settle the regions around the cities of Novgorod and Kiev (today in western Russia and Ukraine, respectively), ruling and mixing with Slavic communities to create a composite culture called Rus (later Russian).

One of the most widely traveled Scandinavian emigrants was the eleventh-century prince and adventurer Harald Sigurdson, remembered as "a handsome man, of noble appearance; his hair and beard yellow. He had a short beard, and long mustaches. The one eyebrow was somewhat higher than the other. He had large hands and feet; but these were well made. His height was five [arm lengths]. He was stern and severe to his enemies, and avenged cruelly all opposition or misdeed."[13] While distinctive, his career reflected wider Scandinavian migration patterns.

In 1030, at age fifteen, Harald fled Norway, after being wounded when his eldest half-brother, King Olaf II (who had converted most Norse people to Roman Catholicism), died in battle. Harald found refuge with the king of Novgorod under whom he served as a warrior. Around 1034, Harald led his growing band of followers down the Dnieper River to the Black Sea and then into Constantinople, where Scandinavians comprised the elite Varangian imperial guard for Byzantine emperors. Harald fought as a mercenary in the Byzantine Empire's conquest of the eastern Mediterranean, much of north Africa, and the Balkans. Other Scandinavian expeditions had already sailed south down the western coast of Europe, around Iberia, and into the Mediterranean, eventually establishing Norman kingdoms in southern Italy and Sicily in the eleventh and twelfth centuries. Thus, immigrants of Scandinavian descent had encircled Europe (and also reached North America), forming mixed communities along its boundaries.

By age twenty-seven, Harald wished to return home with his treasure and claim his royal inheritance. When the Byzantine emperor refused permission for his emigration, Harald escaped. Back in Novgorod by 1045, Harald's riches and martial reputation enabled him to marry the king's daughter, Elizabeth. Returning to Norway, Harald's wealth and fame from his migrations in addition to his royal ancestry and a second wife, Thora, from a powerful Norse family, gained him the throne in 1047 and he became King Harald III.

King Harald's migrations were not over, however. He campaigned futilely for fifteen years to conquer the Danes and ascend their throne as well. In 1066, Harald invaded England, leading a Great Army of a thousand warriors in three hundred longships. But Harald was defeated and killed by the newly crowned Saxon king, Harold Godwinson.

Harold's bloody victory, however, weakened him and he lost his kingdom and his life three weeks later to another invader of Norse descent, King William of Normandy (r. 1066–87). Although relatively small in number, these Norman immigrants seized the landed estates of the established Anglo-Saxon elite, replaced them, and imposed their culture on the local population, eventually producing the English nation.

While Norsemen mastered the coasts and rivers of western and eastern Europe, Mongols used the land to expand out of Central Asia and conquer the surrounding settled communities. Marco Polo, a Venetian merchant who traveled to China in the late thirteenth century, described Mongol transhumant nomadism, the practice of seasonal migration between regions: "The Tartars [Mongols] never remain fixed, but as the winter approaches remove to the plains of a warmer region, to find sufficient pasture for their cattle; and in summer they frequent cold areas in the mountains, where there is water and verdure, and their cattle are free from the annoyance of horse-flies and other biting insects." He further explained, "During two or three months they go progressively higher and seek fresh pasture, the grass not being adequate in any one place to feed the multitudes of which their herds and flocks consist."[14]

The constant militant migrations of the Mongol horde particularly impressed Marco Polo:

> Their huts or tents are formed of rods covered with felt, exactly round, and nicely put together, so they can gather them into one bundle, and make them up as packages, which they carry along with them in their migrations upon a sort of car with four wheels. . . . Besides these cars they have a superior kind of vehicle upon two wheels . . . drawn by oxen and camels [which] convey their wives and children, their utensils, and whatever provisions they require. The women attend to their trading concerns, buy and sell, and provide everything necessary for their husbands and their families; the time of the men is devoted entirely to hunting, hawking, and matters that relate to the military life.[15]

When the Mongols sought luxury goods unavailable in their own herding and hunting economy, they traded with the settled communities of China. If Chinese rulers excluded them from peaceful access, Mongols made raiding incursions. An occasional *dzud* (a snowy cold winter following a summer drought) denied animals grazing year-round and thus forced Mongols to emigrate in large numbers from their homeland. Once in motion, they often continued moving outward, often under a charismatic leader; the most successful and famous of these rulers was Genghis Khan (r. 1206–27), who would unify feuding Mongol clans.

According to Marco Polo, Genghis Khan "was beloved and revered as their deity rather than their sovereign and as the fame of his great and good qualities spread over that part of the world, all the Tartars [Mongols], however dispersed, placed themselves under his command."[16] Leading this militant migration, Genghis Khan penetrated the Great Wall and defeated the north Chinese kingdoms. His successive victories enabled him to incorporate ever more steppe communities, including Turkic-language speakers, into his highly mobile armies, which totaled some one million men. He also innovatively combined the light horse cavalry tactics of the steppes with siege technology learned from the Chinese. His armies proved almost unstoppable as he and his sons conquered from Korea and north China across Central Asia to Afghanistan, northern Iran, the Black Sea, and eastern Russia, creating the largest land empire in history.

The Mongols reportedly considered clearing these conquered lands of the settled population, thus creating grassy steppes that suited their herding lifestyle. But the Mongols recognized the truth of the Chinese proverb that a steppe invader could "conquer on horseback but could not rule on horseback."[17] Therefore, in order to enjoy the wealth and luxury goods produced by settled Chinese farmers and artisans, the Mongols taxed rather than exterminated their Chinese subjects.

The Mongol Empire caused massive movements of people. Soldiers, their wives, and other camp-followers joined the Mongol armies, willingly or perforce. Hundreds of thousands of people fled Mongol depredations, causing secondary migrations by people impacted by these refugees. An Englishman who had been seized and carried along by the Mongols as they invaded Hungary reportedly described them in 1243: "They ride fast bound unto their horses [and] are excellent archers. . . . Vanquished, they ask no favor, and vanquishing, they shew no compassion. They all persist in their purpose of subduing the whole world under their owne subjection, as if they were but one man, and yet they are more than millions in number."[18] Mongols settled as rulers over these conquered lands and recruited officials from conquered kingdoms to administer their vast territories. Under Mongol rule, merchants and travelers moved across Eurasia along more unified and protected transportation corridors.

Genghis Khan's male heirs divided and extended his conquests. The Kipchak Khanate (circa 1240–1502, also known as the Golden Horde) ruled the western steppes and Russia and plundered into

Europe (reaching Vienna in 1241). The Il-Khan dynasty (1256–1335) ruled Iran and Anatolia, with incursions into the Levant and India. The Yuan dynasty (1271–1368) ruled China, with invasions into Vietnam and other parts of Southeast Asia. The first two of these states became Muslim and the third Sinicized, all absorbing the administrative and cultural traditions of the local communities they ruled. But there were limits on Mongol power and their seaborne assaults on Java (1293) and Japan (1274, 1281) failed.

The migrations caused by the Mongols inadvertently led to the spread of the disastrous Bubonic Plague, or "Black Death" (*Yersinia pestis*, transmitted by fleas carried by rodents), which caused pandemics across Eurasia and north Africa. In some regions, half the population died. People fled urban plague spots for the countryside. But immigrants took advantage of lands and jobs left vacant by the many dead. For Europe, which suffered the Black Death from 1347 to 1353, this proved a crucial phase in its long migration history.

Following the fifth-century collapse of the western Roman Empire's barriers to migration, many nomadic groups settled in Europe's newly accessible regions. Many rival barons emerged who hereditarily held their lands from the king "in fee" (*feudum*) in exchange for their feudal oath of loyalty and obedience and with their obligation to serve him with military followers when required. These barons depended on a manorial farming system that kept peasants bound as serfs to the fields around their lord's manor house. Because these serfs could not legally emigrate, their masters could coercively extract their labor and production. But Europe's almost constant warfare also meant massive migrations, especially by armies, and then by the people fleeing them.

Around 800, the charismatic Charlemagne (Charles the Great, r. 768–814) created the Holy Roman Empire by raising his own armies and incorporating the forces of his feudal barons. Some cities had become "free," meaning they were governed directly by the emperor rather than being subject to a local baron. However, various rival kings and barons subsequently reasserted their power, using much of their income to hire mercenary soldiers. Their roving armies attracted many camp followers and displaced many refugees.

During the ecological Medieval Warm Period (circa 900 to circa 1200), agricultural productivity in many parts of northern Europe increased. Communities developed and disseminated new technologies, including the iron plow and improved methods of deforestation and swamp draining. All these changes produced surpluses that enhanced trade and enabled the rise of market towns.

Recognizing the value of international commerce and the rising political influence of English and foreign merchants, King John (r. 1199–1216), through the Magna Carta of 1214, declared, "All merchants may enter or leave England unharmed and without fear, and may stay or travel within it, by land or water, for purposes of trade, free from all illegal exactions, in accordance with ancient and lawful customs."[19] Across Europe, municipalities, groups of cities (including the northern Hanseatic League, twelfth to seventeenth centuries), and urban guilds negotiated tariff and legal agreements with local and distant rulers. They also set regulations for their citizens, both those who were born there or who had immigrated. Increasing population density made cities unhealthy, causing high death rates; new immigrants, however, arrived to replace each city's dead.

Migration also became a prerequisite for some types of economic and social improvement. The growing prosperity and opportunities offered by cities attracted carpenters, stonemasons, and other skilled workmen, who built houses, cathedrals, civic buildings, and defensive walls. In order to qualify as master craftsmen, many artisans traveled for years as journeymen, learning from various teachers. Especially from the twelfth century onward, Europe's renaissance in learning fostered universities to which students and teachers migrated and where others came to serve, feed, and clothe them.

The University of Bologna, the first in Europe, dates its origin to 1088. In 1224, Holy Roman Emperor Frederick II (r. 1220–50) established the rival University of Naples. To recruit students to his university, Frederick promised: "We have therefore decided that in the most pleasant city of Naples there should be teaching of the arts and of all disciplines, so that those who are starved for knowledge will find it in our own kingdom, and will not be forced, in their search for knowledge, to become pilgrims and to beg in foreign lands. . . . We invite the students to such a laudable and great task."[20] Clearly, the emperor was enticing immigrant students to study in Naples and persuading local ones not to emigrate to Bologna.

To make coming to his university attractive for students and faculty, the emperor assured them: "We will allow you to live in a place where everything is in abundance, where the homes are sufficiently spacious, where the customs of everyone are affable. . . . To them we offer all useful things, good conditions . . . and offer prizes to those who are worthy of it. . . . We assure the students, wherever they come from, that they will be able to come, stay and return without any risk."[21] The emperor also promised fine living, low costs, and financial aid: "The best houses will be given to them, and their rent will be at most two ounces of gold. . . . There will be loans given to students, based on their needs." Other European institutions also stimulated individual, group, and mass migrations.

The Roman Catholic Church formed a vast transcontinental arena in which priests, monks, nuns, administrators, workers, soldiers, and pilgrims circulated within its widespread establishment, including whole cities and territories it ruled. Further, to make converts, Catholic missionaries traveled overland across Asia. Many Christians made pilgrimages, the greatest of which was to Jerusalem. European Christian pilgrims traveling to the Holy Land entered into peaceful or violent exchanges with the various communities living along the way or within Jerusalem.

Herman, a thirteenth-century historian and Catholic Benedictine Abbot of Nieder-Altaich, Bavaria, sympathetically recounted the armed pilgrimage to Jerusalem by 12,000 Germans in 1064. In the Balkans, they had to endure "constant danger from [Slavic Christian] thieves and brigands." Next, in Constantinople, they faced Greek Orthodox Christian and imperial Byzantine "arrogance." Then, they entered the Holy Land, which was "occupied by a most ferocious tribe of [Muslim] Arabs who thirsted for human blood."[22] But, these Catholic pilgrims acknowledged that the Muslim ruler of Cairo, the Fatimid Caliph Ma'add al-Mustansir (r. 1036–94), protected them in the Holy Land. During this pilgrimage, most survived their ordeals, reached their goal, and returned home safely.

Many Roman Catholics believed Muslim control over Jerusalem and the rest of the Holy Land was sacrilegious. Some Christian pilgrims protested both to Pope Urban II (r. 1088–99) and to the Greek Orthodox Byzantine emperor Alexios I (r. 1081–1118) that they could not make this pilgrimage or live freely in the Holy Land. Simultaneously, Emperor Alexios requested military assistance from the pope against both the Muslim Seljuk Turks who surrounded him and also against Catholic Norman rulers from southern Italy who fought him in the western Balkans. In 1095, Pope Urban preached and wrote letters promising absolution from sin to all Catholics who went to recapture the Holy Land. Eventually, some 60,000 to 100,000 Catholics, mainly from France, Flanders, Loraine, and the Rhineland, responded in what would later be called the First Crusade.

But many local Christians dreaded this massive armed migration by crusaders. Byzantine princess Anna Komnene, an historian and daughter of Emperor Alexios, wrote, as the First Crusade approached her Constantinople: "For the whole of the West and all the barbarian tribes which dwell between the further side of the Adriatic and the pillars of Heracles [Gibraltar], had all migrated in a body and were marching into Asia . . . like many rivers streaming from all sides . . . they were advancing towards us."[23]

She noted that this advancing multitude included both warriors and peaceful pilgrims: "Frankish soldiers were accompanied by an unarmed host more numerous than the sand or the stars, carrying palms and crosses on their shoulders; women and children, too, came away from their countries. . . . And such an upheaval of both men and women took place then as had never occurred within human memory." She then bemoaned how some crusaders inhumanly devastated her Christians: "The Normans numbering ten thousand . . . behaved most cruelly to all. For they dismembered some of [our subjects'] children and fixed others on wooden spits and roasted them at the fire, and on persons advanced in age they inflicted every kind of torture."[24] She and other Byzantines feared that European adventurers were only using the Crusade as a means to conquer her father's Byzantine Empire. Nonetheless, a tension-filled alliance between her father and these first crusaders captured Jerusalem in 1099. Many Muslim rulers in the eastern Mediterranean recognized the diversity of these Christian immigrants—some hostile, some potential allies.

Sultan Saladin (r. 1174–93) had Kurdish ancestry and had immigrated to Egypt. There his family and an army of 10,000 *Mamluk*s (Muslim warriors, many of them slaves of Circassian origin) overthrew the Fatimid Caliphate and established their own Ayyubid dynasty (1174–1341). During the crusades, some European immigrants settled in the Holy Land among Muslims, Jews, and other Christians. Saladin allied with some Europeans against others and recaptured Jerusalem in 1187.

Usama ibn Munqidh, who immigrated from Shaizar, Syria, in the early twelfth century, was a poet, warrior, and official under Saladin. He described his personal experiences with European immigrants (whom he collectively called Franks): "There are some Franks who have settled in our land and taken to living like Muslims. These are better than those who have just arrived from their homeland, but they are the exception, and cannot be taken as a typical."[25]

For Usama, the Europeans, no matter how friendly, were pretentious and wrongly assumed that European culture was superior:

> A very important Frankish knight . . . had come on pilgrimage and was going home again. We got to know one another, and became firm friends. He called me "brother" and an affectionate friendship grew up between us. . . . He said to me: "My brother, as I am about to return

home, I should be happy if you would send your son with me" (the boy . . . was about fourteen years old . . .), "so that he could meet the noblemen of the realm and learn the arts of politics and chivalry. On his return home he would be a truly cultured man."

Horrified by the idea of entrusting his son to Europeans, Usama none-theless displayed his superior civility by politely refusing the offer:

A truly cultivated man would never be guilty of such a suggestion; my son might as well be taken prisoner as go off into the land of the Franks. I turned to my friend and said: "I assure you that I could desire nothing better for my son, but unfortunately the boy's grandmother, my mother, is very attached to him, and she would not even let him come away with me without extracting a promise from me that I would bring him back to her."[26]

Usama thereby saved his son from the dishonor of emigration to Europe.

The Crusades were not simply armed pilgrimages or invasions by Christianity against Islam but rather included far more complex migration patterns. Various non-Catholic and Jewish communities in Europe also suffered from crusades. And within a few centuries, most European

*The Knights Hospitallers of Saint John began in Jerusalem around 1023 and was dedicated to aiding European Christian religious immigrants to the Holy Land. After the First Crusade, however, they became a religious and military order, fighting to capture and rule the Holy Land for Christianity. This photograph from 1936 shows one of their best-preserved castles, Crac des Chevaliers, now on the Syrian border near Lebanon.* Photo by the American Colony (Jerusalem) Photo Department, courtesy Library of Congress Prints and Photographs Division, LC-M32-7599-B settlers in the Holy Land had return-emigrated to their homeland or that of their ancestors.

After dramatic population rises over preceding centuries, the European population had suddenly fallen due to the mid-fourteenth-century Black Death. Consequently, there were more opportunities available for the survivors. In particular, the shortage of laborers meant that they rose in value relative to the amount of productive land and infrastructure. Across much of Europe, serfs who escaped from their rural masters and lived in a city for more than a year became free. Permanent serfdom gradually gave way to quit-rent, where peasants could legally purchase their freedom. Subsequently, free workers immigrated in large numbers to more flourishing farming areas, cities, and armies, all of which increasingly needed skilled and unskilled labor. Long conflicts, including the Hundred Years' War (1337–1453), bound people with shared cultures together under strong rulers, leading to the emergence of European nation-states, including England, France, and Spain. Thus, many Europeans were on the move even as settled societies developed in scale and complexity and with strong bonds with their land.

The diverse communities of the Americas developed in isolation from those in Eurasia and Africa from the submergence of Beringia until the late fifteenth century (with the exception of the brief encounters between Amerindians and Scandinavians). But our common human nature meant there were many similarities in migration patterns as people everywhere adapted to comparable environments. In more fertile regions, some Amerindian communities cleared farmland. In especially productive Mesoamerica and the Andes mountains, larger settled and urban-based states emerged. Like parts of Eurasia and Africa, however, many other regions in the Americas were dry or heavily forested; in these regions various groups continued as nomadic foragers, hunters, fishers, or swidden farmers.

Population pumps also occurred in the Americas. Climatic periods conducive to farming supported growing numbers of people. But when environmental changes occurred, either natural ones (like prolonged drought) or human-made ones (like exhaustion of local soil fertility or desiccation due to deforestation), the local economy declined, leading to emigration. As groups immigrated into new regions, they displaced or subordinated communities already settled or nomadic there.

The Americas, however, also had environmental differences from the rest of the world that led to distinctive developments in both nomadic and settled migration patterns. Throughout the Americas, there were no large animals that could be domesticated and that were suitable for riding or traction. Without beasts of burden, American nomadic communities, like many in Australia and sub-Saharan Africa, could not travel fast or transport much. Nonetheless, migrants on foot often carried high-value raw materials and goods over long distances. Without animals suitable for pulling plows, farming communities in North and South America could only use hoes and other hand tools. In addition, most Amerindian cultures did not develop metallurgy for weapons, tools, or machines, although some used copper, gold, and silver for ornaments. Nor did Amerindian groups use the wheel, even where they knew about it. In contrast, many Eurasian nomadic and settled communities harnessed domesticated animals and extensively used metals and wheels. As elsewhere on the earth, however, the shared experience of migration brought communities together in the Americas.

One of the largest Mesoamerican states, the Aztec alliance, bonded several communities together through their shared cultural traditions of the Nahuatl language and their long southerly migration on foot from their sacred origin, Aztlan. These related groups each endured expulsions by the settled societies they encountered along their journey. Around 1250, one of these migratory communities settled on a swampy island within Lake Texcoco (now the site of Mexico City). There they adapted by developing the technology of floating fields, *chinampas*, on which flourished extremely intensive agriculture, especially maize, beans, squash, and other vegetables. In order to expand their farmlands by preventing the infusion of salty water and to channel in more fresh water, they built elaborate dike and canal systems. As their community prospered, it mixed economically and culturally with neighboring groups. From around 1325, they expanded their settlements into the city of Tenochtitlan and referred to themselves as the Mexica. At its peak in the fifteenth century, this city alone supported some 300,000 inhabitants, including many immigrants from surrounding regions.

The Mexica also expanded their political power, creating a king, or *tlatoani*, to lead them. They organized an alliance with other cities, exchanging royal women in political marriages. These allied powers induced or forced many surrounding communities to immigrate to their cities, to accept them as overlords and submit tribute, or to move away. Like many states around the world, Aztecs imported captured enemies as slaves, who evidently had few rights, not even including the right to life. To the south, along the Andes, the expanding Inca Empire was also integrating people into its economy and realm. The trans-Atlantic arrival of European conquistadors near the end of the fifteenth century, however, would soon terminate these fragile empires and redirect the migrations of people on all continents at an unprecedented scale.

## CHAPTER 3

# Migrations Start to Reconnect the World, 1450 to 1750

By 1450, the nomadic Roma people, popularly known as Gypsies, had migrated over much of western Asia and virtually all of Europe. About a thousand years earlier, a small group of their ancestors had spread out from northwest India to roam over Iran and Armenia. Then one branch moved across north Africa and another into the Balkans. Various families specialized in particular occupations such as tin smithing, spoon making, and trading; most Roma converted to either Islam or Christianity. The Balkan branch circulated in that region for two or three centuries before persecutions and enslavement produced later periods of emigration across Europe to the Atlantic coast. The Roma now number eleven million in Europe alone, mostly in Romania and Bulgaria, and many retain their traditional migratory role outside of the mainstream of settled societies.

Historically, the Roma did not preserve written records. But they do usually marry only within their community, so their genetic and cultural heritages reveal their collective movements. Distinctive features of their DNA and their Romany language are shared with communities in Punjab (today divided between Pakistan and India). As migration routes of Roma branches diverged, small genetic mutations occurred and dialectical variations in their spoken language developed that mark that branch's particular movements. Wherever they traveled, bands of Roma remained a distinctive minority, often marginalized by the surrounding society. In contrast, other, more militant nomadic groups dominated the communities into whose lands they migrated.

The longstanding Central Asian population pump, when combined with the dynamism of Islam, generated waves of martial emigration outward by various nomadic Turkman, Uzbek, and other Central Asian steppe communities. Gradually, they added new technologies—including gunpowder for firearms and artillery—to their traditional mobile horse-mounted light cavalry armed with powerful reflex bows. Between 1450 and 1550, various Muslim Turkman groups proved particularly successful in conquering south into Asia's more fertile lands. There, they intermingled with the settled societies of Anatolia, Iran, and India to produce the massive Ottoman, Safavid, and Mughal empires, respectively.

In 1451, at age nineteen, when his father died, Fatih Sultan Mehmet II "the Conqueror" inherited leadership of his Ottoman Turkish clan and its principality at Edirne (today in western Turkey). Turkman herders had for centuries emigrated from Central Asia and established themselves in Anatolia and the surrounding regions. Mehmet, traveling tirelessly, mobilized other Turkish kingdoms behind him. At age twenty-one, Mehmet conquered Constantinople, terminating the once vast Byzantine Empire. This city, linking Europe and Asia, remained the Ottoman capital for the next five centuries. Before his death in 1481, Mehmet had attacked Belgrade (1456) and captured Otranto on Italy's southeast tip (1480).

Over the next two centuries, the Ottoman Empire spread over much of eastern and central Europe, the southern and eastern Mediterranean, the Arabian peninsula, and Iraq. Other empires founded by other Turkmans remained land-based. But the Ottomans, in addition to their technologically advanced army, projected their power through an extensive navy, often using war-galleys rowed by slaves.

The family of Admiral Sidi Ali Reis migrated in the late sixteenth century from the Black Sea region to serve as high officials under Ottoman sultans. Sidi Ali himself wrote treatises on astronomy and navigation, including a book on the astrolabe, and later a travelogue about the many lands he explored. In 1553, the sultan appointed him admiral of the Egyptian fleet. These ships had earlier sailed down the Red Sea to drive the Portuguese from the Indian Ocean but, after some initial success, had been forced to take refuge at Basra, Iraq. There, Sidi Ali refitted the remaining fifteen galleys and fought the Portuguese fleet, further damaging his vessels. Then, driven for weeks by a cyclone, his fleet wrecked at Daman on India's northwestern coast. Sidi Ali led the survivors overland up the Indus River and eventually back to the Ottoman capital. Despite the loss of his fleet, the sultan treated him with honor until his death in 1563.

Constantinople (renamed Istanbul in the nineteenth century) became under the Ottomans one of the world's most highly diverse and cosmopolitan imperial cities. Many religious and ethnic communities immigrated, attracted to its wealth and power. To manage this diversity

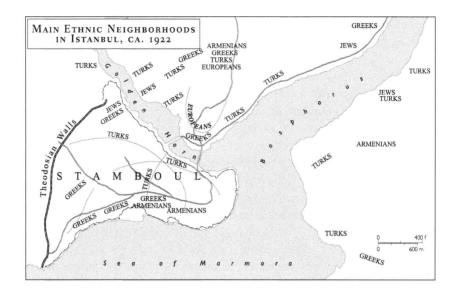

Main Ethnic Neighborhoods in Istanbul, ca. 1922

of subjects, the Ottomans gave a degree of internal autonomy to many of these ethnic nations, or *millet*.

The Ottoman state also used *sürgün* (forced migration) as political policy. In 1490, the Ottomans compelled 3,000 artisans, mostly Armenians, to relocate from Tabriz to the imperial capital. The Ottomans also encouraged Muslim Turks to immigrate into the Balkans (especially to today's Albania and Kosovo), binding that region to Ottoman rule and driving back or converting Christian Serb inhabitants.

Ottoman sultans sought to counterbalance the Turkman nobility in their administration, army, and harem by importing non-Muslim slaves who became dependent aliens with no bonds to the surrounding society. The most skilled or fortunate of these slaves could rise high in the imperial service. A female slave could gain power as Queen Mother if her son inherited his father's Ottoman imperial throne. But, because slaves could not legally pass on property, a male slave could not establish his own dynasty to rival that of his master.

Starting in the fifteenth century, the sultan levied *devşirme* (boy tax) on his Christian subjects in the Balkans: every four or five years, one boy was taken from every five or more households (depending on the manpower needed). Over two centuries, about 200,000 boys were thus taken from their families. The Ottomans then schooled them in Turkish language and culture and assigned each to a branch of the imperial administration. Some became state-regulated Greek Orthodox Christian clergymen but the most promising converted to Islam and served in the

*A Venetian noblewoman sold by pirates into the Ottoman imperial harem who rose to become Queen Mother Safiya commissioned the construction of "New Mosque" in 1597. A Slav (from today's Ukraine) sold by Mongols into the harem who rose to become Queen Mother Turhan Hatice completed it in 1665. This mosque's massive but elegant structure dominates the Galata Bridge over the Golden Horn inlet in Istanbul.* Photo courtesy of Wai Wah Sung

imperial administration as scribes, officials, or soldiers. The latter eventually formed the world's first major professionalized regiments, the Janissaries (New Troops): all wore the same distinctive uniforms, lived in official barracks, received regular salaries, trained to march in step to martial music, and mastered the most innovative and effective cannon and other firearms available. In 1632, however, the Janissaries unsuccessfully attempted a coup against the Ottoman sultan, which led to the formal end of devşirme. East of the Ottomans, their most powerful rival was another Muslim empire with Central Asian roots.

In Iran, the Safavid dynasty (1501–1736) amalgamated nomadic herding Turkman and settled farming Persian Tajik cultures. The founder, Shah Ismail (r. 1501–24), at age fourteen inherited the status of *Pir* (Master) of a Persian-based Shi'ite Sufi religious order and also the throne of Azerbaijan, a regional kingdom. Despite their ties to Central Asia, the Safavids claimed descent from the Prophet Muhammad, implying immigrant Arab ancestry as well as prestige in Islam.

Over the next century, the Safavids spread their rule across Iran and the surrounding regions. Iranian merchants ventured to China, India, the

Levant, and Europe. The Safavids recruited skilled Persian administrators to govern their growing territories. Much Safavid military power depended on steppe warrior-style cavalry, especially composed of *Qizlbash* (Red-Heads, from the red insignia in their turbans), who were Persian-speaking Turks and disciples of the Safavid Sufi order. To counterbalance these Turkic forces, the Safavids captured or purchased thousands of Christian boy-slaves—mostly Georgians, Armenians, and Circassians—whom they converted to Shi'ite Islam and trained as their household guards and cavalry. After Safavid expansion westward was stopped at the battle of Chaldiron (1514) by the Ottomans, who used heavy artillery and massed infantry with muskets, the Safavids amalgamated those military technologies as well.

The Safavids made controlling migration into a state policy. Herding and trading nomadic Turkmans were difficult to tax, so the Safavids tried to settle them. The Safavids also forced about 3,000 Christian Armenian families of artisans and merchants to migrate to Isfahan, their magnificently rebuilt capital, and another five hundred Christian Armenian families to Shiraz, where they established a wine industry. Additionally, the Safavids shifted various non-Persians into northern frontier areas, thus creating a living barrier against Central Asian Uzbek nomads. Occasionally, as when they removed hundreds of thousands of Turks, Armenians, and Georgians from their western boundary with the Ottomans, the Safavids implemented "scorched earth" tactics in which they hindered invaders by forcing all inhabitants to emigrate and destroying all their resources.

After the Safavid empire collapsed, another Turkman warlord conquered Iran: Nadir Shah (r. 1736–47), born into a Qizlbash clan. He brutally forced whole communities, including Armenians, to emigrate from his less-well-controlled western borderlands to his core province of Khorasan. Following his assassination, some of these forced emigrants remained; others return-migrated to their homelands or emigrated to more promising lands. Armenians spread throughout much of Eurasia, producing their extensive trade diaspora network.

For many Central Asians, the settled lands to the south seemed alien places, but ones they had the right to invade and rule. The first Mughal emperor, Babur (r. 1526–30), felt entitled to an empire due to his descent from both the Mongol emperor Genghis Khan (r. 1206–27) and the Turkman emperor Timur/Tamerlane (r. 1370–1405). At age twelve, Babur inherited the throne of a small Central Asian city-state, Farghana, but was soon exiled by his Uzbek rivals and his own relatives. He then wandered as a homeless refugee until age twenty-one, when he and his small band of personal followers captured Kabul.

Eventually, Babur decided to conquer India (known as Hindustan, "land of the Hindus"), which was attractive for its wealth but unpleasant for its monsoon climate and lack of melons. As Babur described in his Turkic-language autobiography, *Baburnama*, India seemed utterly foreign: "I had never seen a hot climate or any of Hindustan before. . . . A new world came into view—different plants, different trees, different animals and birds, different tribes and people, different manners and customs. It was astonishing, truly astonishing."[1] Babur then defeated the Muslim Afghans ruling the Delhi Sultanate and many Hindu regional rulers across north India, thus establishing the Mughal Empire (1526–1858). Babur's descendants eventually extended Mughal rule over virtually all of South Asia, more than one million square miles containing two hundred million people, about two-thirds of them Hindus.

Tensions remained between nomadic and settled ways of life. The Mughal imperial family sought to retain some of its Central Asian nomadic identity by making frequent imperial processions among its several capitals and through its vast provinces, conquering and hunting as they traveled. The Mughals continually encouraged immigration from Central Asia, Iran, and Arabia by Muslim warriors, officials, and scholars. But the Mughals also extensively Indianized their administration and occasionally married brides from Hindu Rajput (royal) regional dynasties. Thus, much of the mtDNA of the Mughal family was from Hindu mothers, although their Y-chromosome descended from Timur. The Mughals built an extensive land-revenue collection administration that combined Persian and Indian technologies to extract taxes from the settled farmers who composed the bulk of their subjects. But herding peoples on India's plains and *adivasi*s (aboriginals) moving around in its extensive (but shrinking) forested areas proved frustrating for Mughal armies and officials to find, control, and tax. As Mughal armies of hundreds of thousands of soldiers and camp followers conquered their way southward across the central Indian Deccan plateau, they faced resistance from local rulers and some African immigrants in their path.

The trans-Saharan and Indian Ocean slavery routes had long existed, forcibly emigrating roughly fourteen million Africans to Asia, more than would cross the Atlantic. Further, the general conditions of slavery differed in these two systems. Slaves in the Atlantic world usually were legal property, with few rights. In contrast, slaves in north Africa and Asia had some legal and customary rights, were often respected for their individual skills, and had the possibility of rising to power.

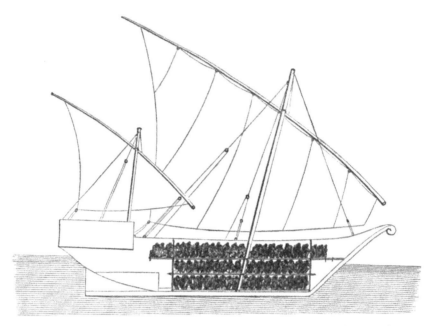

*Dhows have for centuries used the seasonal monsoon winds to sail across the Indian Ocean, sometimes carrying enslaved Africans to markets along its shores. In 1868, British captain George L. Sulivan of HMS* Daphne *captured this dhow with 156 slaves aboard north of Zanzibar, drew this diagram, and then freed them.* From George L. Sulivan, Dhow Chasing in Zanzibar Waters and on the Eastern Coast of Africa; Narrative of Five Years' Experiences in the Suppression of the Slave Trade *(London: Sampson Low, Marston, Low, & Searle, 1873)*

One emancipated African slave of the late sixteenth century, Chapu, rose high in the government of his new central Indian home, the Ahmadnagar Sultanate. Born in the Ethiopian highlands, Chapu was raised by his family in their indigenous "pagan" religious tradition. The neighboring Christian Ethiopian kingdom frequently raided these highlands for slaves, whom it sold to pay for imports brought by merchants sailing across the Indian Ocean. Muslim Arabs also hunted these highlands for slaves. Between the fifteenth and eighteenth centuries, slave takers forcibly exported some 10,000 to 12,000 slaves annually from highland Ethiopia.[2]

Like many others, Chapu endured being sold, perhaps multiple times, in the Arabian peninsula before being imported to Baghdad. There, his Arab owner trained him in military sciences, converted him to Islam, renamed him Ambar, and then resold him at age twenty-two along with a thousand other slaves. His new owner was the chief minister of the Ahmadnagar Sultanate, named Genghis Khan. He was himself a former

Ethiopian military slave who had earned his freedom and risen to power. When Genghis Khan died four years later, his widow freed Ambar in a customary act of Islamic piety.

Like Chapu-turned-Ambar, most emancipated Ethiopian immigrants into India lost connection with their homeland. Further, relatively few Ethiopian female slaves were imported into India. Hence, like most of his fellow African immigrants, he married an Indian. The community produced by such combinations of African and Indian biology and culture called itself Sidi and continues in western India today.

Ambar used his military training to fight the invading Mughal Empire and restore the partly conquered Ahmadnagar Sultanate. His successes drew followers who grew to an army of 50,000 men, including 10,000 other Ethiopians (some enslaved and some free). He was so accomplished that he earned the honorific title *Malik*, or Lord. He wed his daughter to an Ahmadnagar prince whom he then enthroned in 1600. When this puppet ruler tried to oppose him, Malik Ambar reportedly assassinated his son-in-law and installed a more compliant five-year-old Ahmadnagar prince. After Malik Ambar died of old age, his son, Fath Khan, succeeded him as chief minister. But, a decade later in 1636, Ahmadnagar fell to the southward-advancing Mughals. Elsewhere in Eurasia, other immigrant groups were also expanding their rule.

Slavs had settled as farmers in eastern Europe even before the end of the Roman Empire, assimilating people from other cultures, both fellow immigrants and already settled communities. The Russian state of Moscow (including Scandinavians who had settled there) took the political lead and incorporated other Slavic cultures, like the nomadic east Slavic Cossacks. From the late fifteenth century onward, Russian rule extended east into Asia, sporadically pushing back Mongol, Uzbek, and Turkman nomadic groups. The Russian crown advanced its frontier by encouraging Slavic trappers, hunters, and fur traders to emigrate to those sparsely populated territories. Russian rulers also encouraged Slavic farmers to move to these borderlands by giving them homesteads there. By the mid-eighteenth century, imperial Russia had extended settler and military colonies across northern Asia all the way to the Pacific coast and beyond to Alaska.

Russians also consolidated their rule over various Slavic groups in eastern Europe, including in the Ukraine and Caucasus regions, in rivalry with expansive Hungarians, Germans, and Scandinavians. Further, the Russians pushed south against the Ottomans. But Russia simultaneously used serfdom in the Russian homeland to prevent peasants from leaving noblemen's estates (until serf abolition in 1861). Other empires also attempted to control migration across and within their boundaries.

The Chinese Ming dynasty (1368–1644) sought to outlaw emigration by sea. From 1433, Ming and later emperors periodically reissued the following *Hǎi Jìn* (Sea Ban) edict: "All officers of government, soldiers, and private citizens who clandestinely proceed to sea to trade, or who remove to foreign islands for the purpose of inhabiting and cultivating the same, shall be punished according to the law against communicating with rebels and enemies, and consequently suffer death by being beheaded."[3] This edict, although rarely effectively enforced, lasted until 1893. The Ming also forbade outsiders from entering, except as tributary diplomats. But Chinese officials along the coast found both these policies difficult and personally unprofitable to enforce. Thus, many Chinese men (and fewer women) emigrated to Southeast Asia seeking employment and some overseas trade continued. Then, from the sixteenth century onward, Chinese coastal and merchant groups began working in cooperation, as well as competition, with arriving Europeans, thus gradually integrating the Chinese economy into the growing world system.

Within its borders, the Ming Empire encouraged various kinds of migrations. Elite men throughout the empire assembled to take an examination in the Confucianism classics; a high score secured entry into the imperial bureaucracy. During their careers, imperial officials rotated through posts throughout China. Normally they could not serve in their native region, lest they favor their own community. To prevent the creation of personal ties elsewhere, they were regularly transferred among provinces, thereby making them always outsiders. The Ming enhanced imperial communication by establishing relays of couriers and aided the movement of its civil and military administration by means of well-maintained imperial roads and canals. The growing trade along these transportation links also integrated and stimulated the Chinese economy, increasing rural mobility and especially rural-to-urban migration. The Ming also compelled and enticed vast numbers of laborers for its massive building projects, like Beijing, their rebuilt capital.

As did most Chinese rulers, the Ming especially sought to resist Central Asian nomadic raiders along their land borders by forcing and encouraging large numbers of Han Chinese to settle military and farming colonies there. Some 700,000 Han moved to the empire's southwest frontier alone. The Ming also tried to stabilize their northern and western land boundaries to control both raiding and immigration, by rebuilding and extending the Great Wall to over 13,000 miles long. Despite

*Various Chinese dynasties have built, extended, and guarded the Great Wall to mark their boundaries and protect their territory against Central Asian invasions. But, as the power of the Qing dynasty declined during the early twentieth century under pressure from internal rebellions and foreign invasions by Japan, the United States, Russia, and several other European nations, it abandoned the Great Wall, as seen in this 1907 photograph.* Photo by Herbert Ponting

these Ming efforts, the pressures by steppe peoples to enter China eventually proved unstoppable.

The herding Manchu people from Manchuria, having conquered Korea, invaded the weakened Ming and established their own Qing Empire (1644–1911), taking over Beijing as their capital. The Qing proved the last major incursion of steppe peoples into China, although other groups would press into China from the sea. Indeed, states around the world were struggling to control emigration and immigration. In Europe, Iberia developed in ways that led to mass as well as individual migrations.

Over time, many diverse ethnic groups settled in Iberian regions, which they then believed theirs. The peninsula, often divided politically into separate kingdoms, had temporarily been brought together under Roman and then Muslim rule. However, gradually over the eighth to fifteenth centuries, Muslim states gave way to expanding and merging Roman Catholic regional kingdoms in the *Reconquista* (the Reconquest). In 1469, the most expansive of the Catholic kingdoms united through the marriage between King Ferdinand II of Aragon and Queen Isabel of Castile, forming the core of the kingdom of Spain. In 1492, their combined armies captured Granada, the last Muslim kingdom in Iberia. Many Muslims emigrated, but those who remained received promises of religious tolerance (although from 1609 to 1614, Spain would deport 500,000 Muslims and *Moriscos*, Muslim converts to Catholicism).

These Spanish rulers sought to make their subjects a single nationality by supporting the Catholic Church's Inquisition from 1478 onward. Individuals were defined according to the "purity of their blood," not just their outward claims to be Catholic. Thus, Isabel (in 1483) and Ferdinand (in 1492) ordered the expulsion of all Jews (numbering 200,000 to 800,000). A Jewish eyewitness recounted this sudden and disastrous deportation: "The [Spanish] King gave [Jews] three months' time in which to leave. . . . They sold their houses, their landed estates, and their cattle for very small prices, to save themselves. The King did not allow them to carry silver and gold out of his country, so that they were compelled to exchange [these] for merchandise of cloths and skins."[4]

About 120,000 of the Jewish refugees sought a new home in the separate Iberian kingdom of Portugal, making a compact with King John II (r. 1477–95) to pay him one-quarter of their property in exchange for six months of refuge in his kingdom. But "this King acted much worse toward them than the King of Spain, and after the six months had elapsed he made slaves of all those that remained in his country, and banished seven hundred children to a remote island [St. Thomas, near Africa] to settle it, and all of them died. Some say that there were double as many."[5] Portugal also supported the Inquisition from 1536 onward.

Many Jewish refugees fled to north Africa, seeking protection from Muslim rulers there. Of these, some "died in the fields from hunger, thirst, and lack of everything. The lions and bears, which are numerous in this country, killed some of them. . . . [Others] returned to Spain, and became converts."[6] These Jewish converts, *Marranos*, later suffered deportation.

Various European Christians also sought to profit from Jewish forced emigrants: "Vessels came from Genoa to the Spanish harbors to carry away the Jews. The crews of these vessels, too, acted maliciously and meanly toward the Jews, robbed them, and delivered some of them to the famous pirate . . . the Corsair of Genoa. In Genoa, the people of the city showed themselves merciless, and oppressed and robbed them."[7]

But others accepted these Jews as immigrants. The Catholic king of Naples, his Jewish subjects, and "even the [Catholic] Dominican Brotherhood acted mercifully toward them." However, after a plague broke out in that city in 1540, the king expelled all the Jews from his kingdom. Some Jewish refugees eventually found a home under the Ottoman sultans: "Those who arrived there the King of Turkey received kindly, as they were artisans. He lent them money and settled many of them on an island, and gave them fields and estates."[8]

Many other European nations also sought to expel people they considered foreigners. From 1290 to 1655, England officially banned Jews. In 1596, Queen Elizabeth I (r. 1558–1603) ordered the relatively few Africans living in England deported because they allegedly took work from Englishmen: "Of late divers blackmoores brought into this realm, of which kind of people there are already here too manie consideringe howe God hath blessed this land with great increase of people of our owne Nation as anie Countrie in the world, wherof manie for want of Service and meanes to sett them on work fall to Idlenesse and to great extremytie; Her Ma[jesty']s pleasure therefore ys, that those kinde of people should be sent forthe of the lande."[9] Indeed, the process of the creation of any religion or nation often causes the expulsion of inhabitants whom the rulers or majority community deem alien immigrants.

Across Europe, new religious ideologies, most notably the articulation of Protestant Reformation Christianity by Martin Luther and the subsequent Roman Catholic Counter-Reformation, led to massive migrations. The most violent movements of people occurred during the Thirty Years' War (1618–48) in central Europe among Protestant and Catholic rulers. Roving armies used new levels of organized warfare that led to the death of one million people and the forced emigration of countless others. To end this bloody fighting many European rulers signed the Treaty of Westphalia (1648), which became the basis for both the nation-state and international diplomacy. This treaty guaranteed the "full Liberty of Commerce, a secure Passage by Sea and Land" for merchants, some freedom of religion, and the right of emigration of subjects to a neighboring state rather than having to convert to the particular religion of the local ruler.[10] Yet, in 1685, the Catholic French king revoked the nearly century-old Edict of Nantes (which had promised tolerance to Protestants), thereby impelling 400,000 French Calvinists (Huguenots) to emigrate, often having to leave their property behind.

Europeans also made mass migrations for diverse social, legal, and economic reasons. The spreading abolition of serfdom freed peasants to leave their land and seek better living conditions elsewhere, on newly available farmland or in cities. Conversely, legal enclosure by rural landlords of what had been village common lands compelled many consequently deprived peasants to emigrate. Expansion of artisan production (especially of new kinds of consumer goods such as fine textiles), ever higher levels of urbanization, and the rise of commercial classes all accelerated the pace and broadened the scale of migrations. Expanding European states also created new forms of global emigration by seizing most of the rest of the world.

The type of European overseas colonization varied by the respective natures of the sending and receiving lands. Some European states had large populations willing to emigrate to "white settler colonies," especially where the local population was scarce or became sparse due to forced expulsion or depopulation from disease, as in the Americas and Australia. However, even in these so-called white colonies, Europeans forcibly imported large numbers of nonwhite African slaves and Asian indentured laborers. In contrast, in much of west and central Africa, few European colonists settled because they could not endure the local environment. In most of Asia, the local population was already substantial, the climate often proved unhealthy for Europeans, and the travel time from Europe by sailing ship could be many months. In those lands, European colonies remained largely nonwhite.

From the fifteenth century onward, Spain and Portugal, followed by other west European countries, sent out conquerors, missionaries, merchants, and settlers to create colonies in Africa, the Americas, and Asia. From about 1440, the Portuguese developed improved ships that sailed faster and carried more cannon in the stormy Atlantic. They also enhanced their navigation technology and accumulated experience, including knowledge of the complex prevailing oceanic wind and water currents that ensured predictable outward and return voyages. The Portuguese crown sponsored maritime explorations that established colonies on Atlantic islands and ever further south along the west African coast. One major Iberian goal was discovering a direct route to the rich lands of Asia, especially since the Venetian Republic and the expanding Ottoman Empire controlled trade routes eastward via the Mediterranean to Asia. In 1492, the Spanish crown commissioned Christopher Columbus—a

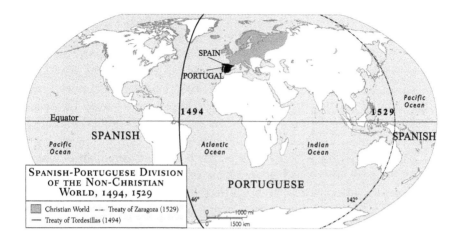

Spanish-Portuguese Division of the Non-Christian World, 1494, 1529

Genoese who had earlier sailed to northern Europe and along the west African coast—to voyage west across the Atlantic to Asia. Instead, he reached the Caribbean and relinked the Americas with Eurasia.

Through the Treaty of Tordesillas (1494), the Spanish and Portuguese monarchs each claimed rule over half of the non-Christian world, with the sanction of the Roman Catholic pope. This treaty drew a line from pole to pole down the Atlantic. "[Then] all lands, both islands and mainlands, found and discovered . . . by the said King of Portugal and by his vessels on [the eastern] side of the said line [belong to him, while] all other lands, both islands and mainlands . . . discovered by the said King and Queen of Castile, Aragon, etc., . . . on the western side of the said [line] . . . shall belong to, and remain in the possession of, and pertain forever to [them]."[11] Later the Treaty of Zaragoza (1529) created another dividing line down the Pacific Ocean. These treaties thus officially gave Brazil, Africa, western Asia, India, Southeast Asia, and Japan to the Portuguese king and the rest of the Americas and the Philippines to the Spanish crown. The Spanish king encouraged many of his European subjects to emigrate to New Spain in the Americas, displacing and subordinating the indigenous population.

The central Mexican Aztec Empire could not comprehend or effectively deal culturally, politically, militarily, or medically with the militant immigration of Spanish conquistadors led by Hernán Cortés. Many Aztecs tried to explain the Spanish arrival by evoking their own religious tradition of migration from the sacred city of Aztlan, and thus identifying the arriving Spaniards as divinities, whom they should worship and placate. When warfare ensued, starting in 1519, the numerically larger but less powerfully armed Aztec armies were shredded by merciless Spanish guns, swords, metal armor, horse-mounted cavalrymen, and war-dogs. Within two years, the fragile Aztec political alliance shattered as some Amerindian rival and subordinated communities guided and supported the Spanish invaders. Spanish conquistadors similarly defeated other Amerindian communities across central America, in the southwest of North America, and along the Pacific coasts of both Americas. Since Amerindians had no immunities to inadvertently imported European diseases, their population plunged from roughly one hundred million at contact to only about two million a century later.

Many surviving Amerindians perforce labored for Spanish immigrants. The Spanish royal government under the *encomienda* system "entrusted" Amerindians to Spanish officials and elite settlers. The Spanish grant holder could take tribute from these assigned Amerindians, in the form of work or property, in exchange for nominally instructing them in Spanish, converting them to Roman Catholicism, and protecting them. This forced labor system proved so harsh it offended even some Spaniards. Over the mid-sixteenth century, the crown partially replaced it in the Americas (and the Philippines) by the *repartimiento* system, under which each adult Amerindian (or Filipino) male had to annually labor two months at low wages for Spanish settlers.

Many Iberians responded to the push of impoverishment at home (made worse by inflation due to the inflow of American silver and gold) and to the pull of promised wealth in a colony. By the mid-eighteenth century, some 700,000 Spaniards had emigrated to New Spain and the Philippines and about 500,000 Portuguese emigrated to its Brazilian, African, or Asian colonies. Their private letters illustrate chain migration, because prosperous (but often lonely) immigrants persuaded others to join them.

On March 8, 1574, immigrant Alonso Ortiz described his new life in Mexico City to his distant wife, Leonor González, who had remained in Spain with their children. Before emigrating, he had been hard-pressed by creditors but he proved to the Spanish crown that he was Catholic, not of Muslim or Jewish descent, and thus worthy of immigration into New Spain. When Ortiz arrived, he started a tannery because the expanding colonial society needed to turn its growing herds of cattle into meat and leather. Initially, Ortiz had to do the onerous manual labor of butchering and skinning himself. Other Spanish immigrant tanners were reluctant to let their few trained Amerindian employees work for a rival and he was not prominent enough to receive an assignment of Indian laborers. Within a year, however, Ortiz managed to hire six to eight Amerindians to slaughter 1,000 to 2,000 animals annually and cure their hides, leaving him to supervise the purchasing, processing, and selling. Soon, to expand his business, he added a Spanish partner, who contributed capital and a valuable, skilled African slave.

Legally, married Spanish colonists must have their wives with them. Although this was usually not enforced, Ortiz wrote his wife expressing his personal loneliness, entreating her and their children to join him:

> I endured difficulties before God guided me here, to the place where I am and will remain. . . . I will make good use of the health with which God has blessed me, and that this time not be lost, I have worked, and I continue to work, with great care; I try not to spend money wastefully, and I earn much more than I need to make ends meet. There is, in all this, only one thing wrong, and that is that I do not have you and the children with me.[12]

He also sent her (secretly so his Spanish creditors would not intercept it) 150 pesos, about three months' profit, "to feed you, to pay for the preparation of your belongings and provisions for the trip, and for all other related business . . . if you decide to come." Further, he sent his power of attorney so she could sell his property in Spain and promised to send 100 hides for her to sell and placate his creditors so they would allow her to emigrate.

Immigrant María de Carranza had settled in Puebla de los Angeles (between Veracruz port and Mexico City) with her husband, a textile mill owner. On October 2, 1589, she wrote enticingly and entreatingly to her brother:

> Desired and beloved brother of my heart:
>
> [Why do] you want to stay there in that poverty and need which people suffer in Spain. I ask you for the love of God to spare me such pain from your absence, and yourself such necessity, when I have the means to give you relief. Do be sure to come [to Mexico] quickly now, and don't make your children endure hunger and necessity.
>
> [Mortgage my houses in Spain] and invest all except what you need for travel in fine cloths, in Rouen [French] and Dutch linens . . . because here it is very expensive.[13]

In addition, she urged her brother to recruit even more immigrants: "Do everything in your power to bring along with you two masters of weaving coarse woolens and carding, for they will profit us greatly, and also a candlemaker, who should be an examined journeyman and good at his trade. . . . I will fulfill whatever you agree to; I will pay their passage and any debts they have when they arrive." She concluded, "As to my beloved daughter Mencía Gómez, I have reserved a very rich marriage [here] for her."[14]

Indeed, much of the wealth that such Spanish immigrants gained in the Americas went to purchase textiles, food, and other products from France, the Netherlands, England, and elsewhere in northern Europe, stimulating their economies and population movements. Northern European ship-wrights learned to build merchant vessels with even greater carrying capacity for bulk cargo, passengers, and cannon that increased the volume, pace, and powerful effects of migration throughout their spreading empires.

Especially from the seventeenth century onward, northern European merchants created commercial joint stock corporations that sought profit by negotiating from their own governments trade monopolies and colonies in the Americas, Africa, and Asia. Such corporations included the Dutch West India Company (founded 1621), the English Royal African Company (1660), and the East India Companies of the English (1600), Dutch (1602), Danes (1616), French (1660), and Swedes (1731). These corporations accumulated international capital for investment in ships and purchases. They also hired European merchants, military officers, and officials to emigrate to profit from, conquer, and govern their many and often vast colonies. While these corporations tended not to form white settler colonies, the cumulative number of Europeans could be substantial: in the seventeenth and eighteenth centuries, the Dutch East India Company sent one million Europeans (many of them emigrants from German states) to Asia, especially to Indonesia.

North America's Atlantic coast received various white settler colonies organized by entrepreneurs and corporations. William Penn, an English Quaker (a member of the Society of Friends), was granted Pennsylvania by the English royal family as payment for personal debts in 1681. He then sold a 15,000-acre tract to a German company in Frankfort, which created Germantown, Pennsylvania. In 1683, this Frankfort company hired Francis Daniel Pastorius, a university-educated German lawyer, poet, antislavery abolitionist, and beekeeper, to lead their settlement.

Pastorius recalled the diversity of his fellow emigrants, including his nine servants:

> My [shipmates crossing the Atlantic] consisted of many sorts of people. There was a doctor of medicine with his wife and eight children, a French captain, a Low Dutch cake baker, an apothecary, a glassblower, a mason, a smith, a wheelwright, a cabinet-maker, a cooper, a hat-maker, a cobbler, a tailor, a gardener, farmers, seamstresses, etc., in all about eighty persons besides the crew. They were not only different in respect to age (for our oldest woman was sixty years of age and the youngest child only twelve weeks) and in respect to their occupations . . . but were also of such different religions and behaviors that I might not unfittingly compare the ship that bore them hither with Noah's Ark, but that there were more unclean than clean (rational) animals to be found therein. In my household I have those who hold to the Roman, to the Lutheran, to the Calvinistic, to the Anabaptist, and to the Anglican church, and only one Quaker.[15]

After his arrival, Pastorius found Amerindians more cultured and European settlers less civilized than he had expected: "As to [Pennsylvania's] inhabitants, I cannot better classify them than into the native and the engrafted. For if I were to call the former savages and the latter Christians, I should do great injustice to many of both varieties." Many companies have sought to profit by encouraging migration; Pastorius's German employers used for publicity his *Positive Information from America, Concerning the Country of Pennsylvania by a German Who Traveled There* (1684).

Many would-be European emigrants lacked enough money for the voyage. Two-thirds of the Irish, English, Scots, French, and German immigrants to North America by the end of the eighteenth century went as indentured laborers. They borrowed the cost of their passage and signed indentures, contracts that bound them to repay the advance by working for a specified number of years at low wages plus often minimal lodging and food. Many European immigrants, having served the term of their indenture, settled as free colonists or chose to return to their original homeland. This system echoed the European guild system in which people apprenticed to master craftsmen for fixed terms of training at little or no wages before they could take to the road as credentialed journeymen. In contrast, however, many indentured laborers in America received little vocational training and their lives as manual laborers could be hard. Many did not survive the term of their indenture.

On March 20, 1623, Richard Frethorne, an Englishman living near Jamestown, Virginia, wrote his parents regretting his decision to immigrate by indenture:

> [We indentured] must work hard both early and late for a mess of water gruel and a mouthful of bread and beef. . . . [Our] people cry out day and night—Oh! That they were in England . . . and would not care [losing] any limb to be in England again, yea, though they beg from door to door. For we live in fear of the [Amerindian] enemy every hour, yet we have had a combat with them . . . and we took two alive and made slaves of them [as was our] policy, . . . for our plantation is very weak by reason of the death and sickness of our company. . . . I am not half [or] a quarter so strong as I was in England, and all is for want of victuals; for I do protest unto you that I have eaten more in [one] day at home than I have allowed me here for a week.[16]

Seeing most of his fellow indentured immigrants die around him, he lamented his vanishing hopes for a prosperous new life in America:

> There [is] nothing to be gotten here but sickness and death, except [if] one had money to lay out in some things for profit. But I have nothing

at all—no, not a shirt to my back but two rags, nor clothes but one poor suit, nor but one pair of shoes, but one pair of stockings, but one cap, [and] but two [collars]. My cloak is stolen by one of my fellow [immigrants], and to his dying hour [he] would not tell me what he did with it; but some of my fellows saw him have butter and beef out of a ship, which my cloak, I doubt [not], paid for. So that I have not a penny.

He then begged his parents to free him by paying off his indenture in cash or by sending goods that he could sell and repay his debt: "If you love me you will redeem me suddenly, for which I do entreat and beg . . . the answer of this letter will be life or death to me."[17] Many indentured immigrants faced similar harsh conditions.

Gottlieb Mittelberger, a German lay preacher, schoolteacher, and organist, immigrated to Philadelphia in 1750. He described the passage to America:

In Amsterdam the people are packed densely, like herrings so to say, in the large sea-vessels [carrying] four to six hundred souls. . . . During the voyage there is on board these ships terrible misery, stench, fumes, horror, vomiting, many kinds of sea-sickness, fever, dysentery, head-ache, heat, constipation, boils, scurvy, cancer, mouth-rot, and the like, all of which come from old and sharply salted food and meat, also from very bad and foul water, so that many die miserably. . . . Children from 1 to 7 years rarely survive the voyage . . . no less than 32 children in our ship . . . were thrown into the sea.

Immigrants who survived the voyage often had to bind themselves into indenture after their arrival in America: "When the ships have landed at Philadelphia after their long voyage, no one is permitted to leave them except those who pay for their passage or can give good security; the others, who cannot pay, must remain on board the ships till they are purchased."[18]

Mittelberger then explained the process:

Every day Englishmen, Dutchmen and High-German people come from the city of Philadelphia and other places . . . and go on board . . . and bargain with [immigrants] how long they will serve for their passage money. . . . Adult persons bind themselves in writing to serve 3, 4, 5 or 6 years . . . according to their age and strength. But very young people, from 10 to 15 years, must serve till they are 21 years old.

Many parents must sell and trade away their children like so many head of cattle; for if their children take the debt upon themselves, the parents can leave the ship free and unrestrained; . . . such parents and children, after leaving the ship, do not see each other again for many years, perhaps no more in all their lives.[19]

Like many immigrants who found America failed to satisfy their expectations, Mittelberger returned to Germany in 1754 and warned other would-be emigrants what horrors awaited them. However, Europeans continued to emigrate by indenture until the early nineteenth century.

This migration pattern of temporary indentured servitude in America had a parallel in the transportation of European criminals sentenced to work there, often instead of execution. The British government authorized this sentence in 1718 and, over the following half-century, transported 40,000 to 50,000 British convicts to North America; many died during the passage. After the newly independent United States refused to take more British prisoners, the British crown started transporting them to Australia. Europeans, however, were not the only new global emigrants due to European colonialism.

Amerindians, Africans, and Asians also migrated, willingly or perforce, via the new global transportation routes created by European ships. Non-Europeans replaced European seamen who deserted or died (as about half did on voyages to Asia during the seventeenth century) and sailed the vessels back to Europe. Various non-Europeans traveled to Europe as short- or long-term immigrants sponsored or captured by European explorers or entrepreneurs. Europeans sought to impress them with European achievements, to train them as intermediaries serving European goals, and to entertain and edify indigenous Europeans with human specimens from distant and strange cultures. Additionally, non-European wives and employees of Europeans also ventured back to Europe with them. Especially from the seventeenth century onward, small populations of Amerindian, African, and Asian immigrants settled in Europe. Two of the most widely known Amerindians in Europe were Tisquantum (popularly known as Squanto) and Pocahontas.

Squanto, after having peacefully traded with Englishmen from his Patuxet home on the Massachusetts coast, was among twenty-seven Amerindians seized in 1614 by Englishman Thomas Hunt and brought to Spain for sale as slaves. However, Squanto and a few companions claimed Spanish protection from slavery by becoming Roman Catholics. From Spain, Squanto migrated to London where he worked for shipwright John Slany, who was also treasurer of the English Newfoundland Company (founded in 1610). In 1618, Squanto sailed with Slany to Newfoundland but then returned to England before voyaging back to Massachusetts. There, he found that most of his Patuxet community had migrated away or died from the European-originated diseases that killed some 90 percent of Amerindians. Pilgrims, who immigrated on the *Mayflower* in 1620, built their Plymouth colony near his former village.

Subsequently, Squanto sought to find his surviving kinsmen, to assist English settlers in learning Amerindian farming techniques, and to negotiate for them with various Amerindian communities. Squanto himself was captured in 1621 by other Amerindians settled on Martha's Vineyard island. Their leader, Epenow, had himself earlier been seized and brought to England, lived there for three years, and then, on his return home, escaped and fought the English. After Plymouth colony ransomed Squanto, he continued to negotiate on their behalf until his death.

Most Europeans who migrated to the Americas, Africa, or Asia were male and many married or cohabited with women from the local communities they traded with or conquered. Many settlements with mixed biological and cultural ancestry resulted. Some Europeans brought back to Europe their non-European wives and children. Among the most celebrated wives was Pocahontas, a daughter of Powhatan, an Amerindian headman living near the English colony of Jamestown. In 1613, the English kidnapped teenage Pocahontas as hostage for some Englishmen and tools that her father had allegedly seized. During her captivity, she converted to Anglican Christianity with the baptismal name Rebecca and married an English widower and early successful tobacco planter, John Rolfe, with whom she had a son, Thomas, in 1615. Then, she, her English family, and about eleven fellow Amerindians traveled to London. However, Pocahontas never left England, dying in 1617 on the eve of her return. Englishmen likewise brought home with them Asians and Africans.

The Armenian Christian family of Mariam had immigrated to India, probably during the sixteenth century. Her father, Mubarak Khan, rose high in the service of Mughal emperors. After he died and his brothers claimed his wealth, Mariam and her mother were taken into the shelter of the harem of Mughal emperor Jahangir (r. 1605–27) as honored companions to his own wives. When William Hawkins arrived at the Mughal court at Agra in 1609 as the first English ambassador (representing both the English king and the English East India Company), Jahangir enrolled him as a Mughal imperial official and insisted that he marry a wife to manage his household. Since Hawkins swore to wed only a Christian, Jahangir offered Mariam. For Hawkins, her submission made this a highly satisfactory marriage: "Forever after I lived content and without feare, she being willing to goe where I went, and live as I lived."[20]

Two years after their marriage, however, Hawkins lost favor with Emperor Jahangir and, fearing his Portuguese rivals, hurriedly left the imperial court. Breaking his promise to her family that they would not leave India, he and Mariam sailed in a fleet of English East India Company ships east to Java and then west to England in 1612. But Mariam arrived a widow: Hawkins had died aboard along with many other passengers and crew. Soon after Mariam reached London, she married Gabriel Towerson, an English merchant and captain of another ship in their fleet. According to English law, her husband controlled the diamonds she had brought from India and also the cash given her by the East India Company as a "token of their love" for her first husband's service as ambassador.[21]

On the voyage back to England, Towerson had also kidnapped a south African, named Coree, probably from the nomadic Khoisan community. In London, the East India Company then trained Coree as a translator and intermediary with his people. Indeed, after his return to south Africa, Coree assisted the English until the Dutch East India Company executed him in 1627 for aiding their English enemies.

Mariam and her new husband settled in London. After four years there, however, Towerson took Mariam back to India, planning to profit from her connections with the Mughal court and her Armenian community. As appropriate for her elevated status, she was served on the voyage by English attendants: a "gentle waiting woman," Mrs. Frances Webb, a female companion, Mrs. Hudson, and several other English servants. However, after their arrival at the Mughal court in 1617, Towerson's personal arrogance alienated his countrymen and hers. Eventually, he left India, abandoning Mariam with little money and only a young English boy as her remaining servant. For years thereafter, the East India Company listened sympathetically to her petitions for alimony but could not compel Towerson to support her. Indeed, at his new post in Maluku (today in Indonesia), Towerson clashed with the Dutch and was tortured and executed by them in 1623 along with nine other Englishmen, one Portuguese, and nine Japanese employees of the English East India Company. The English, however, were not the only ones importing non-Europeans.

The Roman Catholic Church brought to Europe converts from throughout the world, including scholars, translators, and missionaries-in-training. Some eventually returned home carrying knowledge of Europe; others remained there the rest of their lives. Such immigrants had a range of experiences, including the following Chinese Catholic converts: "Michael Alphonsius" Shen Fu-tsung arrived in 1682, met the kings of France and England, and taught Chinese language and culture at Oxford University. He died in 1691 during the voyage home. "Lionne Arcadio" Huang immigrated at age twenty-three in 1702 via London and Rome to Paris to translate and catalogue Chinese books in the French Royal Library. In 1714, he married a Frenchwoman, Marie-Claude

Regnier, and had a daughter, but died in Paris soon thereafter. "Louis/ Luigi" Fan Shouyi went, in 1708, at age twenty-six to Rome as part of a diplomatic mission from the Chinese emperor to the pope, visiting Brazil and much of southern Europe on his way. He learned Latin and was ordained a priest. After his return to China in 1719, he wrote his memoirs, *Shen jian lu* (1721), and personally informed the Qing emperor about Europe, its geography, and curious customs. "John/Giovanni" Hu Ruowang converted to Catholicism, went in 1722 to France and Italy as a scribe of Chinese books, but never adapted to local customs and was confined in a lunatic asylum for twenty months. Finally, after four years in Europe, he returned to China.[22] Apprehending the disruptions that European colonialism inevitably caused, some societies tried to isolate themselves from the expanding world system.

Japan's shoguns proved to be among the world's most successful governments in excluding immigration and controlling migration within its boundaries. The Tokugawa clan under Ieyasu organized a coalition of other daimyo who triumphed and he seized control as shogun in 1600. Each successive hereditary shogun then worked to unify Japan under his close supervision, compelling hundreds of leading daimyo to migrate biennially between his capital at Edo (later renamed Tokyo) and their provincial domains.

While fine roads and coastal shipping enabled people to move and trade throughout the Japanese islands, the shoguns effectively cut off Japan from the outside world. Portuguese merchants and missionaries had been immigrating to Japan since 1543; indeed, about half a million Japanese had converted to Catholic Christianity. The shoguns determined to suppress these foreigners (whom they called "southern barbarians") as well as Japanese Christians by expelling the former and compelling the latter to renounce Christianity or die. In 1635, the shogun had the emperor issue the Closed Country Edict, which ordered (among other provisions):

1. Japanese ships are strictly forbidden to leave for foreign countries.
2. No Japanese is permitted to go abroad. If there is anyone who attempts to do so secretly, he must be executed. The ship so involved must be impounded and its owner arrested, and the matter must be reported to higher authority.
3. If any Japanese returns from overseas after residing there, he must be put to death.[23]

Shoguns wanted to keep the sacred land of Japan pure and their subjects out of the reach of outsiders.

Yet, shoguns also wanted to import precious goods and keep themselves informed about world events. Hence, they allowed a few Chinese merchants to import silk and a few Dutch East India Company Europeans to enter, but only allowed them to live on the artificial island of Dejima in Nagasaki harbor, which was built in 1641 to keep these temporary immigrants off Japan's sacred soil. Although some unofficial emigration continued, Japan remained outside of the world system (until after 1852, when Commodore Matthew Perry brought an American war fleet and forced Japan to participate again). Other communities proved less able to resist the disruptive effects of European colonialism.

Before the arrival of European ships along Africa's coasts, sub-Saharan Africans followed a range of migration patterns. Many nomadic communities, including the herding Fulani community (also known as the Fula or Fulbe), had accepted Islam and profited from trans-Saharan trade into the Sahel. They extended southward, where they mixed with other Muslim communities to create several Hausa-Fulani sultanates in northern Nigeria.

Other west Africans, who spoke one of the Bantu family of languages, had long been developing their farming technology, including through improving metallurgy. Their new developments enabled their culture to expand east and south, incorporating various local peoples. In regions particularly fertile, rich in minerals, or strategically located for trade, expansive states emerged, including the Yoruba (in today's Nigeria), the Ashanti (in today's Ghana), and Zimbabwe (in southeast Africa).

Many expanding sub-Saharan African states conflicted with each other and subordinated or forced out communities living along their frontiers. People captured in war or taken for tribute, as well as those sold for debts or sentenced for crimes, often became domestic slaves. Such enslaved men and women retained some rights, often living as subordinate members of their owner's family. Land was generally available to any free member of the community who could farm it, so it had no commercial value. But slaves did. Male slaves often proved harder to control and domesticate, so they tended more often to be sold to brokers and to be forcibly exported regionally or into the intercontinental Islamic world. But European laws and practices of ownership of slaves as chattel, or property, profoundly altered the lives of millions of Africans enslaved for profit and exported over the Atlantic.

The Portuguese crown from the fifteenth century onward, followed by other European powers, established a series of armed trading posts along Africa's west and southeast coasts. Initially, they purchased or seized small numbers of slaves for importation into Europe, usually as prestigious servants who embodied their owner's wealth. But, from 1510 onward, Europeans imported ever larger numbers of Africans into the Americas as unskilled and skilled manual laborers. These imported Africans replaced local Amerindians whose populations plummeted due to invasive European and African diseases, including malaria and yellow fever. Simultaneously, expanding plantation economies, particularly sugarcane, required huge numbers of workers, especially males. Europeans paid for slaves with weapons and other goods, intensifying slave-capturing raids and wars among African kingdoms.

European commercial demand enhanced in Africa the monetary value of slaves and rerouted some of their forced migrations to the west African coast instead of north across the Sahara or east across the Indian Ocean. Some entrepreneurial African communities along the west African coast profited as intermediaries collecting and transporting slaves from the interior to European coastal outposts and ships. From there, enslaved Africans (about one-third from west Africa) were forcibly exported to American markets. Portuguese slave ships predominated until 1640 but were thereafter surpassed by English ships in numbers of voyages and of slaves carried.

European colonial empires initiated new global arenas of migration. Almost all humans on earth either participated in or resisted this new Eurocentric world system. Wherever in the Americas, Asia, Africa, or Australia that Europeans established colonies, European immigrants and their rule, including their imported crops, diseases, weapons, products, and cultures, profoundly dislocated local communities, leading many to migrate away. But European traders, settlers, officers, and officials also attracted indigenous people to translate, guide, serve, fight for, and otherwise collaborate with them. Gradually the economies and societies of much of the world shifted; many of the largest cities outside of Europe today were originally created by European colonialism. By 1750, the world's population was still less than one billion people, only one-seventh of what it is today, but migration had become a global phenomenon as never before in world history.

## CHAPTER 4

# National and International Migrations, 1750 to 1914

Little Ephriam and Acona Robin, two young brothers of the leading Robin John family of Old Town on Africa's west coast, were among the earliest slaves to write about their own lives. They recounted their capture in 1767 and subsequent traumatic migrations through the Caribbean, Virginia, England, and then home. Their Efik community of Ibibio speakers had migrated to the Cross River estuary of the Biafra region (today in southeast Nigeria) two centuries earlier, settling as fishermen and traders of fish and salt into the interior. When Portuguese and then English ships arrived seeking slaves, the Efik and other coastal communities supplied them—at least 3.5 million enslaved people unwillingly emigrated from this region of west Africa. Some leading Efik families sent their sons to England for education in language, accounting, and customs, so as to be able to negotiate more expertly. Arriving European slave traders gave advance payments of cash, luxury goods, and weapons to Efik traders, who sometimes left their own sons aboard ship as hostages until they seized or purchased and delivered the contracted slaves. To obtain slaves, the Efik made two- or three-week-long expeditions up the Cross River, using up to eighty-foot-long canoes, each carrying some 120 men, with cannon in the bow and stern, paddled by their own house slaves. Many such expeditions were needed to fill a single slave ship. In the year 1767 alone, 15,674 slaves unwillingly emigrated from the Cross River, including these two Efik brothers.

During heated negotiations over a trade dispute, English slavers kidnapped Little Ephriam and Acona Robin and killed another brother, while their neighboring Efik rivals massacred many other Old Townsmen. During the enslaved brothers' passage across the Atlantic to the Caribbean, one-fifth of the slaves aboard died; only 272 survived to be sold in Dominica, a British island colony. There, a French physician purchased the brothers; Acona Robin reported, "we was treated . . . upon ye whole not badly." However, they believed a British ship captain who promised to return them home and fled to his vessel. Instead, the deceitful captain seized and sold them in Virginia. Their next owner proved harsher; Acona Robin wrote, "he would tie me up & whip me many times for nothing at al then some times be Cause I could not Dress [prepare] his Diner for him not understanding how to do it . . . he was exceeding badly man ever I saw." After five years, when this owner died, they fled to another British captain who likewise falsely promised to return them home. Instead, he brought them to Bristol, England, and prepared to resell them. However, using their knowledge of English culture and law, they negotiated their freedom, went to school, converted to Methodist Christianity, and wrote in English describing their lives. After seven years away, they returned home, although most enslaved Africans never would.[1]

One of the most numerous and destructive forced migrations directly caused by European colonialism was the brutal exportation of approximately twelve million Africans as slaves across the Atlantic. Up to one-third of these unwilling emigrants died aboard or soon after sale in the Americas. Of the survivors, about five million were sold in Brazil, three million in British North America and the Caribbean, and one-and-a-half million in Spanish America.

French, British, Portuguese, and Dutch merchants sold another half million African and Indian slaves in the Indian Ocean region. Most slave-ship captains treated these enslaved African people like commodities—inhumanely transported and sold for the highest possible profit. Captains practiced either "tight packing" (which increased both the number of slaves crammed into the ship as well as their death rate) or "loose packing" (which loaded fewer Africans and expected a higher proportion of them to survive the voyage).

This Middle Passage, along which many European and American seamen and merchants as well as African slaves migrated in roughly 35,000 slave-ship voyages, formed the second leg of the Atlantic triangular trade. On the first leg, from Europe to west Africa, European ships brought European manufactured products, cloth from India, and rum from New England, among other goods. On the third leg, European and American ships carried to Europe sugar from the Caribbean and Brazil; tobacco, rice, and indigo from southeastern North America; and other raw materials for Europe's burgeoning industries and consumers.

Even more than most other immigrants, enslaved Africans in the Americas struggled to retain their cultural identities. Most endured the disorientation of their vicious capture; their hellish transportation to remote, overseas lands without realistic prospect of return home; their degrading sale as objects; their brutal life as manual laborers; often limited or no contact with Africans of their own ethnicity; and the constant threat of resale away from whatever family or community they had managed to create. Many of the slaves had sophisticated skills, including expertise in rice growing and drumming, and we can see their cultural resilience in many of their arts, their Vodun religion, and their periodic uprisings. European property laws, however, meant that slaves and their children had few rights or realistic ways to obtain their freedom.

African slaves in Boston described their forced emigration and current pitiful condition through a futile appeal in 1774 to the British governor of Massachusetts for protection against their colonial America owners:

> We were unjustly dragged by the cruel hand of power from our dearest friends and some of us stolen from the bosoms of our tender Parents and from a Populous Pleasant and plentiful country and Brought hither to be made slaves for Life in a Christian land. Thus we are deprived of every thing that hath a tendency to make life even tolerable, the endearing ties of husband and wife, we are strangers too for we are no longer man and wife than our masters or mistresses think proper married or unmarried. Our children are also taken from us by force and sent many miles from us where we seldom or ever see them again, there to be made slaves of for Life which sometimes; is very short by Reason of Being dragged from their mother's Breast.[2]

Few slaves were able to liberate themselves and even fewer to write about their unwilling migrations, as did Little Ephriam and Acona Robin. But those who did write aided the abolition movement by demonstrating their literacy and humanity to white Europeans and Americans. Olaudah Equiano stands among the most widely read ex-slave.

An Igbo born in the mid-eighteenth century, Olaudah Equiano movingly described enslavement and forced migration from the Biafra coast by African slavers like the Robin John family.[3] Equiano then detailed his own migrations as a slave in the Caribbean and North and South America, sailing as far as the Arctic and around the Mediterranean. Saving diligently from his own trading, he purchased his freedom at age twenty-one in Montserrat, a British Caribbean colony: "I who had been a slave in the morning, trembling at the will of another, was become my own master, and completely free. . . . The fair as well as black people immediately styled me by a new appellation, to me the most desirable in the world, which was Freeman."[4] Nonetheless, as he migrated, he still had to struggle to escape re-enslavement.

Equiano eventually settled in Britain, converted to the Church of England, and became a professional orator and author, publishing his autobiography, *Interesting Narrative of the Life of Olaudah Equiano*, in 1789. In 1792, he married a white Englishwoman, Susan Cullen, with whom he had two daughters. Calling himself "The Oppressed Ethiopean," he worked tirelessly with other British abolitionists to shift public sentiment against slavery and to protect the "millions of my African countrymen, who groan under the lash of tyranny in the West Indies."[5]

In 1787, Equiano received the British government's official appointment as Commissary of Provisions and Stores for the Black Poor going to Sierra Leone. Following the American Revolution, many escaped or liberated slaves like him immigrated to London. Britons of the Committee for the Relief of the Black Poor and the British government sponsored the emigration of more than four hundred colonists to west Africa (where most had never been) to start the colony of Sierra Leone as a place where former slaves could build their own community. Some British authorities wished to clear London's streets of homeless or other undesired people, so, in addition to poor blacks, some white British women and at least one Asian were also shipped to this colony. Creating Sierra Leone, however, displaced indigenous African communities. Further, due to corruption and inefficiencies by the British organizers, which led Equiano to protest and then be dismissed, the first settlement of 1787 did poorly. However, after new immigration by 1,200 free black people, mainly from Nova Scotia, Canada, this colony became permanent in 1792. (Sierra Leone became an independent nation in 1961.)

African former slaves and other abolitionists convinced growing numbers of Europeans about the inhumanity of slavery. Additionally, economic shifts made international slave trading less profitable. Hence, various governments abolished this trade, including Denmark in 1803 followed by Britain (whose ships had carried the most African slaves) and the United States in 1807. In 1815, at the diplomatic conference called the Congress of Vienna, many other European countries agreed to end international slave trading. Subsequently, the British navy (and, to a lesser extent, the American and other navies) intercepted slave ships and released their human cargo on the coast of Africa. They did not, however, try to reunite them with their original communities.

But slavery remained legal in many parts of the world, as long as owners kept their human property within national boundaries. The brutality of legal slavery ended in British colonies in 1843, French colonies in 1846, Brazil in 1888, Saudi Arabia in 1962, and Mauritania in 1981. In the United States, several northern states abolished slavery, starting with Vermont in 1777, but these new abolition laws led many white owners to move their slaves to southern states, which still recognized slaves as property. For these slaves, forced migration southward meant increased hardship.

Migration for slaves and former slaves could, however, mean liberation. Some black and white Americans believed blacks should leave America and move to Africa as their racial homeland. In the Back to Africa Movement, former slaves and their descendants, sponsored by the American Colonization Society, emigrated to create the west African colony of Liberia in 1821 (which became an independent nation in 1847). Return-migration of African Americans to the continent of their ancestors would continue in various forms. In the decades leading up to and during the American Civil War (1861–65), about 160,000 slaves freed themselves by illegally migrating to Mexico, to Amerindian lands, or else north along the seacoast or inland through the Underground Railway network of way-station refuges to free states or into Canada. Only in 1865 did the Constitution's Thirteenth Amendment end slavery in the entire United States.

A growing number of other countries around the world largely followed the nation-state model, which increasingly controlled movement within and across their legal borders by both citizens and noncitizens. This led to the development of the concept of international migration, that is, migration passing over demarcated and policed national boundaries. Further, governments developed the capacity to identify and mobilize their citizens collectively; the French Republic was one of the first nation-states to do so.

Following France's 1789 revolution, the Committee for Public Safety proclaimed *Levée en Masse*, or general conscription:

> From this moment until that in which the enemy shall have been driven from the soil of the Republic, all Frenchmen are in permanent requisition for the service of the armies. The young men shall go to battle; the married men shall forge arms and transport provisions; the women shall make tents and clothing and shall serve in the hospitals; the children shall turn old linen into lint; the aged shall betake themselves to the public places in order to arouse the courage of the warriors and preach the hatred of kings and the unity of the Republic.[6]

This mobilized a national army of 800,000 citizens, with the rest of the population supporting them, thus replacing the older royal model army comprised mostly of professional mercenary troops, who were often imported.

Under the command of an immigrant from Corsica, French emperor Napoleon Bonaparte (r. 1804–15), vast imperial armies spread across continental Europe and overseas. These massive armed migrations included soldiers conscripted from many nations and produced "total war" that uprooted entire societies. In the First Spanish War of Independence (1808–14), thousands of Spanish civilians left their homes to fight in guerrilla, "little war," bands against Napoleon's crushing invasion. In 1812, Napoleon invaded Russia with 600,000 soldiers in addition to huge numbers of camp followers. The Russian czar mobilized equally vast armies and scorched the earth, removing all people, shelter, and food, before advancing (and then retreating) Napoleonic armies. Each campaign created uncounted numbers of refugees.

France also sent many soldiers, officials, missionaries, merchants, and settlers to conquer, govern, and profit from its overseas colonies. At various times, France ruled much of north and west Africa, Madagascar, Canada, French Guiana, Vietnam, Laos, Cambodia, and various Indian Ocean, Caribbean, and Pacific islands. After conquering Algeria in 1830, 50,000 white French immigrants displaced much of the indigenous Berber population from the best farmlands. The French colonial empire competed in the Americas, Africa, and Asia with the even larger British Empire, each moving large numbers of soldiers, sailors, and civilians around the world in global conflicts. These rival empires exchanged colonies, and the people living in them, back and forth in war and in the peace negotiations that followed.

Bound and free British emigrants settled on every habitable continent to create the largest empire by population and geographic extent in world history. English kings had long been moving subordinated groups around within the British Isles. From the late sixteenth century, English kings impelled Protestants from Scotland and England to immigrate to farms, called plantations, in northern Ireland, displacing Irish Catholics. The English crown at various times encouraged or forced the emigration of many different religious and social groups who appeared alien or threatening.

Many British emigrants were free but others were prisoners. The 1787 First Fleet transported to southeastern Australia more than 500 male British convicts, about 200 female convicts, almost 20 of their children, and about 350 free persons. By the 1830s, about 3,000 British convicts arrived annually in Australia, many others dying during the voyages. By 1868, when the practice of criminal transportation ended, over 160,000 men and almost 25,000 women prisoners had emigrated this way.

Alongside these forced emigrants from Britain, many more went to Australia voluntarily. Many Britons, other Europeans, and some Asians settled along Australia's coasts or moved inland, creating expansive sheep ranches, farms, and mines, driving back aboriginal peoples, and reducing their population by 90 percent. By the late nineteenth century, about four million Europeans had migrated to Australia and New Zealand. Britons also emigrated to North and South America, both within the British Empire and beyond it. Today, about 60 percent of Canadians, 20 percent of U.S. citizens, and 100,000 Argentinians claim British ancestry.

Over the eighteenth and the nineteenth centuries, Britain also extended nonwhite colonies over large parts of Africa and Asia. Fewer Britons immigrated to these lands. Nonetheless, European colonial rule dislocated most of the local populations through wars of conquest and the extensive economic consequences that followed. European colonizers also created new intermediate classes of local people who reoriented themselves toward European culture and migrated accordingly. Thus, European empires formed intercontinental arenas for voluntary migration by the colonized.

Many diverse people from British-ruled India migrated throughout the Indian Ocean region and to Southeast Asia—including seamen, servants, clerks, merchants, laborers, and the wives and children of British men. During the eighteenth and early nineteenth centuries, thousands of Indian soldiers, termed *sepoys*, fought in British wars in China, Southeast Asia, Africa, west Asia, and Europe. Britain also forcibly transported thousands of Indian prisoners throughout its empire in Asia, both removing them from their home societies and using them as cheap labor in other colonies. Additionally, by the mid-nineteenth century, tens of thousands of Indians had migrated to Britain, most as servants and seamen; many more would follow in subsequent decades.

One Indian Muslim, Sake Dean Mahomed, described movingly how in 1761, at age eleven, he left his widowed mother in Patna, north India, to join the English East India Company's army:

> The number of [British] Officers passing by our door . . . attracted my notice, and excited the ambition I already had of entering on a military life. . . . The notion of carrying arms, and living in a camp, could not be easily removed; my fond mother's entreaties were of no avail. . . . Her disappointment smote my soul—she stood silent—yet I could perceive some tears succeed each other, stealing down her cheeks—my

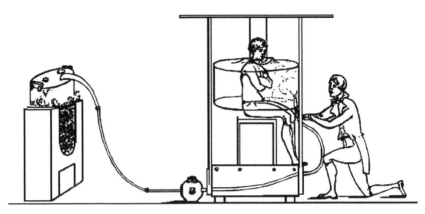

*Some particularly entrepreneurial immigrants from Asia to Europe advertised their exotic origins and distinctive access to "Eastern" knowledge. One Muslim from India, Sake Dean Mahomed, prospered in early nineteenth-century England as an expert practitioner of his original "Indian Medicated Vapour Bath," applying medicine-infused steam to European clients.* From Basil Cochrane, *An Improvement on Administering the Vapour Bath* (London: John Booth, 1809)

> heart was wrung—at length, seeing my resolution fixed as fate, she dragged herself away, and returned home in a state of mind beyond my power to describe.[7]

For fifteen years, he marched hundreds of miles across north India as a camp follower and then soldier. Many other Indian men also left their homes to volunteer for these British-commanded East India Company armies that enabled the British to conquer and rule across India; by the time of his death, about a quarter million Indians were currently enlisted.

At age twenty-five, however, Mahomed resigned from the East India Company Army and immigrated to Cork, Ireland. There, he eloped with an Anglo-Irish woman, Jane Daly, and raised a family. He also wrote and published his 1794 autobiographical travel narrative about his life in India. Once people have made a long-distance migration, they often do so again later in life to become serial emigrants.

Around age forty, Mahomed immigrated to London with part of his family. There, he married another Englishwoman, Jane Jefferys, and started London's first Indian restaurant owned by an Indian. After his restaurant failed in 1812, he moved to the English seaside resort of Brighton, prospering with his bathhouse that featured exotic Asian medical practices. While highlighting his Indian immigrant identity to attract a European clientele, Mahomed also partly assimilated,

*From 1821 to 1843, Sake Dean Mahomed ran his fashionable bathhouse in the*
*English coastal resort of Brighton, making himself famous as the royal*
*"Shampooing Surgeon." But "shampooing" (originally derived from Indian*
*therapeutic massage,* champi) *became, after his death, mere hair wash.*
From S. D. Mahomed, *Shampooing* (Brighton: self-published, 1838)


becoming Anglican and voting in British Parliamentary elections. His
grandsons included a Church of England minister and a prominent
London physician. Although Mahomed made himself a professional
medical man in England, most Asian emigrants migrated as manual laborers throughout the tropics.

With the ending of the intercontinental migration systems of African slavery and European indentured labor, new sources for large
numbers of cheap workers were needed by European-owned sugar
plantations and other colonial enterprises in tropical regions. Europeans and freed blacks generally refused such poorly paid and dangerous
employment. However, periodic famines and political upheavals—
including from periodic El-Niño–related droughts, China's Taiping Rebellion (1851–64), and India's 1857 uprising—drove many Asians to
emigrate as free or indentured labor.

During the nineteenth and early twentieth centuries, twenty million
Chinese emigrated overseas, mostly farmers from southeastern China.
Many intended to be sojourners, temporarily emigrating to make their
fortunes and then returning home to enjoy it. Indeed, most eventually
return-migrated, although few returned rich. Most went as free laborers,
although they often incurred private debts to pay their passage. About

750,000 went as indentured laborers, especially to Southeast Asia and the Caribbean, often with much hardship and few rights. If they broke their indenture, most governments classed it as a criminal act, not a civil contract violation. Owners of the indentures of these immigrants could sell them, as indicated in an 1847 advertisement from a Havana, Cuba, newspaper: "For Sale: A Chinese girl with two daughters, one of 12–13 years and the other of 5–6, useful for whatever you may desire. Also one mule."[8] Nonetheless, unlike trans-Atlantic slaves, the children of indentured immigrants were usually born free, although their parents might indenture them.

Specific regions of India also proved catchments for indentured recruitment and free emigrants. Thirty million Indian emigrants went to work on tropical plantations, including to Ceylon (now called Sri Lanka), Burma (now called Myanmar), Malaya, Fiji, the Caribbean, Mauritius and Reunion islands, and south and east Africa. Many intended to be temporary sojourners or regretted their decision to immigrate and returned home. In the early twentieth century, one-third of Indian immigrants to British Guiana died and many others on-migrated or return-migrated (however, the remaining Indian population there still rose to a plurality by the time of its independence as Guyana in 1966).

As metal-hulled and steam-driven ships replaced wooden sailing vessels, Asian indentured laborers traveled much faster and further, with far lower death rates, than had trans-Atlantic slaves. But the recruitment, passage, and immigrant lives of indentured Asians were still often brutal. The Chinese imperial and British colonial governments occasionally tried to regulate indentured emigration from their territories, as did some governments in the receiving British colonies, the United States, Latin America, and other destinations. Most governments legally required that laborers sign the indenture voluntarily. But recruiters—both Europeans and Asians, including former indentured laborers—sometimes enticed, misled, or forced people into signing the indenture.

"[We] were all beguiled on board the barbarian [American] ship as contract laborers by emigration agents and confined in the hold. . . . After the ship sailed, the said barbarian gave each man in the hold a contract of servitude. If he did not accept he was flogged. . . . More than ten who were sick in bed and could not walk were immediately killed and thrown into the ocean."[9] So testified one Chinese emigrant in 1852 about how he and his more than four hundred fellow recruits from Fujian, southeast China, agreed verbally to work in California, but then were locked into barracks and soon taken aboard an American ship, the

*Robert Browne.* So harsh and murderous was their treatment that these Chinese seized the vessel, killed some of the crew, and escaped onto a small island near Okinawa. After British and American warships recaptured seventy of these men, those governments investigated the illegal recruitment of "coolies," the derogatory label endured by almost all Asian indentured and free immigrants to the Americas and Africa. While most Asian immigrants were men, many of the receiving governments preferred families in order to create more stable and self-perpetuating worker communities.

Immigrants who completed their indenture legally had the option of return passage home, but many chose to stay. About two-thirds of Indian indentured laborers in the Caribbean settled there. Of the rest who returned to India, about one-third again immigrated to the Caribbean, either by signing new indentures or as free workers, still often working on plantations producing sugar for export. Today, there are about twenty-four million people of Indian descent living overseas. Most colonial emigrants went as workers, but a few wealthier ones went as students.

Increasingly, during the nineteenth century, elite men emigrated from European colonies to Europe for their advanced education. Living among Europeans, they learned about the inequalities of global imperialism. Some then returned to mobilize their compatriots for independence.

After both his parents died, sixteen-year-old Simón de Bolívar went in 1799 from Spanish-ruled colonial Latin America to study in Europe before returning to liberate his people. He declared in 1819, "We are not Europeans; we are not [American] Indians; we are but a mixed species of aborigines and Spaniards. Americans by birth and Europeans by law, . . . we are disputing with the natives for titles of ownership, and at the same time we are struggling to maintain ourselves in the country that gave us birth against the opposition of the invaders."[10] His nationalist movement against the Spanish Empire created the nation of Gran Colombia, which in 1830 divided into Colombia, Ecuador, and Venezuela (from which Panama seceded in 1903). However, former colonies that became newly independent nations still remained part of the world system of economics and migration as growing numbers of people migrated to extract raw materials from the earth's oceans and lands, to process them into finished goods in factories, and then to distribute them globally.

From the late eighteenth century onward, tens of thousands of seamen from the United States and other nations made extended transoceanic voyages hunting whales for their oil (used for lighting and lubrication) and baleen (used for men's collar stiffeners, women's corset stays, and buggy whips). Many sub-Saharan Africans, especially after the international slave trade no longer exported them to plantations in the Americas, moved within their own regions to plantations that exported rubber or palm tree oils (used to lubricate machinery, make soap, and cook with) and to mines that exported metals and other minerals. Uncountable numbers of Europeans left farming as it commercialized, mechanized, and dislodged previously stable rural communities, generating surplus emigrant labor. The coal many of these emigrants mined fueled steam-powered machines that supplemented or replaced human, animal, and wind energy for mining, manufacturing, and transportation.

Gathering momentum during the nineteenth century, the steam-powered Industrial Revolution transformed migration patterns first in western Europe, then in North America, and eventually globally. Expanding factories attracted massive numbers of workers; the distribution of their output created far-reaching commercial networks of shippers and venders. Railways more rapidly transported ever more people and freight: within Britain (from the 1830s) and then transcontinentally across the United States (1869), Canada (1885), Siberia (1905), and Australia (1917). Railways also moved underground as subways, in London from 1863 and then in other major cities, enabling urban commuters to live further from their work. Steamships speeded water transport on inland rivers and canals and across oceans. Many imported laborers and engineers shortened sea voyages with interoceanic canals like the Suez (1869) and Panama (1914). Mining and concentrating minerals and other raw materials made the Industrial Revolution possible.

Gold and silver rushes created whole new communities as hundreds of thousands of miners and the men and women who supported and profited from them immigrated to California (1848), Nevada (1849), Victoria, Australia (1851), Fraser River, Canada (1858), Alaska (1880), South Africa (1886), and the Klondike, Canada (1896 to 1899). Other newly discovered mineral deposits, including copper and diamonds, also created massive migrations to previously isolated regions. Many men and women set out as prospectors, miners, and the people who supported them, but only a lucky or plucky few reached their goal and even fewer returned home rich.

After the development of petroleum-powered internal combustion engines for manufacturing and transportation, ever more people migrated for oil drilling, refining, and distributing. In addition to motor fuel, the petroleum industry also produced kerosene for cooking and lighting, plastics, chemical fertilizers, pesticides, and other derivatives that affected people everywhere. Petroleum-powered automobiles, trucks, busses, and trains increased in number, range, speed, and popularity, especially after automobiles were mass produced in huge factories filled with immigrant laborers (including America's Ford Model T from 1908). Hope for a better life elsewhere motivated many emigrants and they could increasingly move more easily and quickly within regions, nations, or intercontinentally.

From the late eighteenth to the early twentieth centuries, vast numbers of Europeans emigrated because their rising expectations or vital needs were not satisfied in their homelands. Multiple disruptions throughout Europe during the Napoleonic Wars (1799–1815), and the periodic economic depressions that followed, convinced many to seek a more promising future elsewhere. Many relocated to cities within their nation or other European lands. But others were attracted by the idea of new opportunities in North or South American and Australian cities and along their mining and farming frontiers. Simultaneously, many governments increasingly sought to control their borders by setting immigration and emigration policies.

The United States determined to encourage immigration by reputedly hardworking and skilled Germans. But the king of Bavaria wished to deter emigration by his productive subjects. Hence, in 1845, they negotiated a treaty that recognized his sovereign right to forbid the emigration of any particular person.[11] This treaty, however, also prevented him from taxing or confiscating the property of any of his subjects whom he allowed to emigrate to the United States. Once naturalized, these immigrants, like all other free American citizens, had the constitutional right to move freely among its states; such freedoms and opportunities attracted many European immigrants unable or unwilling to remain at home.

From the late eighteenth century onward, Europe's agricultural innovations, including crops imported from the Americas, led to significant rises in population, occasionally outstripping supportable levels and forcing emigration. In the mid-nineteenth century, the repeated failure of the potato crop in northern Europe caused the emigration of millions, especially the rural poor. This tuber was an intentional import from America that had become the main staple of many European farmers, sustaining their lives and those of their children, and thus enabling significant population increase. But, from 1845 until 1850, an invasive blight (*Phytophthora infestans*), inadvertently imported from America, repeatedly destroyed up to 90 percent of the potato crop across northern Europe. Many millions starved. More than a million

American society welcomed some European immigrants. A popular American journal published this illustration, entitled "Leaving Old England for America," showing British families and young men sadly leaving home but optimistically coming to begin a new life in the United States. From Harper's Weekly (January 22, 1870)

emigrated from rural highland Scotland. In western Ireland, where tenant farmers had long suffered severely, often from demands by absentee landlords, about one million died and another two million emigrated.

From the start of the potato famine until the early twentieth century, Ireland's population shrank by almost one-half, down to 4.4 million, largely due to famine deaths and emigration. As many Irish emigrated to the Americas as remained in their homeland. But some white Protestant emigrants from Europe, who had earlier settled in the United States and become citizens, tried to exclude these refugee Irish as alien in race, as Catholics, and as impoverished laborers who undercut the wages of true Americans. It took generations of struggle and assimilation for these Irish to gain a measure of acceptance, a pattern endured by many immigrant groups.

Improvements in steamships made the trans-Atlantic passage ever faster and cheaper. However, conditions for poor emigrants paying the least by going "steerage," that is, cabin-less on the lower decks, were difficult and perilous. These vessels were commonly known as "coffin ships"; sometimes 15 percent of the immigrants died before reaching shore. Nonetheless, with better international communication and transportation systems in place, people were able to retain connections with their original homelands and encourage relatives and friends to follow in chain migrations.

The nineteenth century saw huge waves of emigration from across Europe to the Americas, peaking at more than one million annually. During that century, the United States and Canada received at least 9.5 million Christian and Jewish eastern Europeans, 7.5 million Britons (including Irish), 5.5 million Germans, 4.2 million Italians, and 2 million Scandinavians. During the decade following Brazil's abolition of slavery in 1888, about one million Europeans voluntarily emigrated there, mostly laborers responding to the demand for replacement workers. Then, in the first decade of the twentieth century, about 1.5 million Italian workers and farmers emigrated to Argentina and Brazil. Later in life, many European immigrants made return-migrations back to their original homeland, including about half the Italian and Scottish immigrants to the United States. But so traumatic was Irish emigration that relatively few ever returned, however patriotic they might remain about Ireland. Similarly, few Jewish emigrants returned to eastern Europe. These large numbers of immigrants needed places to live, and they either packed densely into cities or displaced earlier settled immigrants or Amerindians.

North American cities expanded dramatically. Due mostly to recent international immigrants, New York City's population multiplied from 800,000 in 1860 to 4,800,000 by 1910. Many North American cities became ethnic quilts, as immigrants settled in particular neighborhoods with others from the same homeland, who spoke their language, cooked their foods, and formed civic associations and voting blocks to protect and advance themselves.

The concept of a transcontinental nation was expressed in the 1840s as America's Manifest Destiny. During the nineteenth century, the United States extended its political boundaries by purchase, diplomacy, and seizure. In so doing, the United States greatly expanded its territories for both long-settled immigrant families and also recent immigrants from overseas. The United States added 2.8 million square miles through purchase from France, Spain, and Russia (Louisiana, 1803; Florida, 1819; southern Arizona, 1853; Alaska, 1867; Guam and Puerto Rico, 1898); negotiation with Great Britain of the Canadian border (1818, 1846); and war with Mexico (the Southwest and California, 1848). Additionally, the United States purchased or annexed many Amerindian lands and the independent states of Texas (1845) and Hawai'i (1898). The United States also temporarily ruled Cuba (1898 to 1902) and the Philippines (1898 to 1946). Each acquisition resulted from, and caused, complex migration patterns.

Individuals and communities of immigrants seeking new lives moved into the newly opened American interior. In 1847, the Church of Jesus Christ of Latter-Day Saints (popularly known as Mormons) made their exodus from Ohio, Illinois, and Iowa beyond the frontier to their "New Jerusalem": Salt Lake City, Utah. By 1869, about 85,000 Mormon pioneers had made this migration, which became a vital foundational event in their community's sacred history. The massive dislocation of the American Civil War (1861–65), during which about three million soldiers left their homes to fight and cuntless civilians were displaced, led many survivors to migrate westward to the American frontier. Immigrants from Europe and Asia to America's Pacific coast also pushed eastward.

Gradually, new transportation, agricultural, and communication technologies, including Conestoga Wagons, railways, canals, steel deep-cutting plows, combine harvesters, and the telegraph, bound what had been frontier communities into the national economy, extracting raw materials and becoming markets for factory-produced goods. The 1890 U.S. Census officially noted the end of this frontier: "Up to and including 1880 the country had a frontier of settlement, but at present the

*East Coast American pioneers and settlers migrating westward needed large, covered, and sturdy vehicles that could be safely hauled by draft animals over rough terrain and protect their cargoes and passengers, even while crossing rivers. The most famous style was the Conestoga Wagon, first developed in the early eighteenth century in Pennsylvania.* From John Omwake, *The Conestoga Six-Horse Bell Teams of Eastern Pennsylvania* (Cincinnati: Ebbert & Richardson, 1930)

unsettled area has been so broken into by isolated bodies of settlement that there can hardly be said to be a frontier line. . . . [The term frontier] cannot, therefore, any longer have a place in the census reports."[12] Thereafter, migration largely occurred to, from, or within America's settled communities.

Immigration from America's coasts imposed not only physical but also cultural displacement on Amerindians. Especially following the United States' 1830 Indian Removal Act, various Amerindian communities in the Southeast emigrated perforce to the Indian Territory (today in Oklahoma). Many people did not survive the journey or their harsh lives in their new lands, called "reservations" after 1851. Some Amerindians forcefully defended themselves against white American incursions.

Black Hawk, a Sauk Indian leader who fought white immigrants and the American Army, finally surrendered in 1832 at age sixty-five. He recalled the experience of losing his community's land:

> We came up to our village, and found that the whites . . . had come, and that the greater part of our corn-fields had been enclosed. . . . Why did the Great Spirit ever send the whites to . . . drive us from our homes, and introduce among us *poisonous liquors, disease and death*? They should have remained on the island where the Great Spirit first placed them. . . . Wherever the Great Spirit places his people, they ought to be satisfied to remain, and thankful for what He has given them; and not drive others from the country He has given them, because it happens to be better than theirs! . . . What *right* had these people to our village, and our fields, which the Great Spirit had given us to live upon?[13]

American society still commemorates Black Hawk's manly bravery, including selling consumer goods emblazoned with his image and naming Chicago's professional ice-hockey team and a military helicopter after him. Similar displacement and assimilation of indigenous people by immigrants, and conflicts among armed immigrants, occurred increasingly over the nineteenth century throughout the world.

South Africa's temperate climate, strategic location for world trade, and agricultural and mineral wealth made it one of the most attractive regions of sub-Saharan Africa for European immigrants. In 1652, the Dutch East India Company made Cape Town a key resupply settlement for European ships passing to and from Asia. Many Dutch Calvinist, French Huguenot, and German Lutheran immigrants settled as farmers there, gradually merging to become ethnic Afrikaners: white Africans with their own language, Afrikaans. Especially from the 1740s, Afrikaners migrated beyond the Dutch colonial frontier into the interior, as herders, traders, and farmers, known as Voortrekkers, "Pioneers," or Trekboers (migrating farmers). After British colonial rule finally replaced the Dutch in 1806, about 12,000 more Afrikaners left on the Boer Great Treks into the interior, where they displaced or subordinated indigenous peoples and founded their own countries: Orange Free State and Transvaal.

At the same time, Zulu and other communities speaking Nguni languages were expanding into this same region as part of the extensive Bantu migrations across central and southern Africa. During the early nineteenth century, the dynamic Zulu chief, Shaka, was particularly effective as a war leader. He mobilized young Zulu men into highly mobile military units organized by age; they served Shaka militarily until he granted them permission to marry and settle in their own homesteads. With each triumph, Shaka incorporated new communities into his forces. Shaka's successors also fought Afrikaners and later British immigrants who entered Zulu lands.

*After his surrender to the United States army, Black Hawk, or in his Sauk name, Ma-Ka-Tai-Me-She-Kia-Kiak, became known in the American popular imagination as the idealized Indian warrior. More than four decades after his death in 1838, a tobacco company used this stylized image of Black Hawk as advertising on the lid of its packaging.* Courtesy Library of Congress Prints and Photographs Division, LC-USZC4-3255

In the adjacent highland region of southern Africa, the Basuto people had settled as an earlier part of the Bantu migrations. Their herding and farming had displaced many of the nomadic Khoisan people who had been living there, perhaps from the beginnings of Homo sapiens. In the mid-nineteenth century, the Basuto further extended their kingdom, brought in European missionaries and political advisors, and negotiated a peace treaty with the British that guaranteed their territories. But Afrikaner settlers claimed Basuto lands, which led to violent clashes.

In 1858, Mark X of Moshweshewe, the Basuto king, explained to the British: "People who had come from [Cape] Colony first . . . called themselves Boers. I thought all white men were honest. Some of these Boers asked permission to live upon our borders. I was led to believe they would live with me as my own people lived, that is, looking to me as to a father and a friend." But Afrikaners did not accept their status as tolerated subordinates to this Basuto chief. Rather, "The Boers then began to talk of their right to places I had then lent to them. . . . The Boers consider all those farms as their own, and were buying and selling them one to the other, and driving out by one means or another my own people."[14]

Initially, the Basuto chief's authority prevailed: "I tried my utmost to satisfy them and avert war. I punished thieves, and sent my son Nehemiah and others to watch the part of the country near the Boers, and thus check stealing. In this he was successful, thieving did cease. We were at peace for a time." But when Afrikaners seized more Basuto lands, warfare erupted: "my people living near farmers received orders [from Boers] to remove from their places. . . . [And] the Boers went further and further day by day . . . massacring my people. . . . I had given orders that no [Afrikaner] farms should be burnt, and my orders were obeyed till my people saw village after village burnt, . . . they then carried destruction among the enemy's homes." The Basuto chief's appeal for British protection only partially succeeded. In 1867, the British Cape government allowed the Afrikaner Orange Free State to seize half of Basutoland. But the British made the rest a protectorate, indirectly ruled through the Basuto king (after British decolonization in 1966, this became the current independent Kingdom of Lesotho, surrounded by the Republic of South Africa).

British immigrants seeking South Africa's agricultural and mineral wealth convinced the British government to import about 300,000 British soldiers for wars against the Zulus (1879) and Afrikaners (1880–81, 1899–1902). The British also mobilized for their armies some of the 40,000 Indians who had immigrated to South

Africa, mostly as indentured laborers. Mohandas "Mahatma" Gandhi, who lived for twenty-two years in South Africa, served himself and assisted in recruiting other Indians to support these British colonial wars. The British, in order to defeat Afrikaner guerrilla soldiers, uprooted 100,000 of their family members into concentration camps, where many died. In 1910, the British incorporated the two Afrikaner states and the British colonies of Cape Town and Natal into the Union of South Africa: a white-dominated, largely self-governing dominion under the British crown (which achieved independence in 1966).

The system of apartheid, which would emerge in South Africa in the mid-twentieth century, had its roots in pass laws dating from 1797 for black Africans and from 1906 for Asians. Under these laws, Africans and Asians in South Africa could not even briefly venture out of their restricted zones unless they carried a passbook that authorized travel, signed by a white man. Ironically, these same Africans and Asians were full citizens of the British Empire and could legally immigrate into Britain, settle, and vote there. While apartheid was an extreme method of restricting internal migration, many governments attempt to regulate the movements of particular categories of people within their borders.

The Russian Empire was the most expansive state in continental Eurasia from the late eighteenth through the nineteenth centuries, ruling eight million square miles at its peak. While a multiethnic state with combined European and Asian identities, the Russian Empire had as its core Slavic culture and the Russian Orthodox Christian Church. However, the imperial Romanov dynasty (1613–1917) itself included non-Slav, non-Orthodox immigrants.

Empress Catherine the Great (r. 1762–96), an immigrant from the German kingdom of Prussia, ruled Russia during one of its most expansive periods. She was born a Lutheran Protestant princess named Sophia in a German-speaking family. At age fifteen, her family sent her to Russia to be married to the future Czar Peter III, who had himself immigrated from a German principality.

She recalled her struggles to make a good first impression in the lavish imperial court: "I had arrived in Russia very poorly outfitted; though I had three or four outfits, I was at the end of the world, and at a court where one changed outfits three times a day. A dozen chemises made up all my lingerie; I used my mother's bed linens." Gradually, as the expected future empress, her role in the court grew:

> Upon my arrival in Moscow, the Empress had given me ladies- and men-in-waiting, who made up my court. [Later], she gave me Russian

ladies-in-waiting so as to facilitate, she said, my active use of the Russian language. This suited me greatly. They were all young, the oldest being around twenty. These girls were all lively, so that from that moment on, I did nothing but sing, dance, and frolic in my room from the moment I awoke until I fell asleep. In the evening after dinner . . . we would play blind man's bluff and all sorts of other games suitable to our age.[15]

In addition to studying Russian, she converted to Russian Orthodoxy and was rechristened Catherine.

While she strongly disliked her future husband, she was determined to succeed. Marriage at age sixteen was the price she was willing to pay: "August 21 [1745] was fixed by the Empress as the date for the ceremony. As this day approached, I grew more deeply melancholic. My heart did not foresee great happiness; ambition alone sustained me. At the bottom of my soul I [believed] . . . sooner or later I would succeed in becoming the sovereign Empress of Russia in my own right."[16] Indeed, only six months after her husband Peter's enthronement in 1762, her supporters deposed and executed him, making Catherine the ruling empress.

Under Catherine, the Russian Empire expanded by 200,000 square miles in eastern Europe and Central Asia. To extend her borders, she encouraged substantial Russian and other Slavic immigration. She also sent massive imperial armies to annex large parts of Poland in 1772 and then much of southeast Europe.

Her government imposed different laws on each of the many diverse communities under Russian rule. While not as favored as Russian Orthodox Christians, Roman Catholics received some protections and rights. Russia's five million Jews, however, could not obtain citizenship, paid heavy extra taxes, and had to live within "the Pale." Created by Catherine, the Pale's boundaries changed over time but its territories are today mostly found in Poland, Ukraine, Moldova, Belarus, Lithuania, and western Russia. Periodically, the Russian imperial government tolerated or instigated pogroms against Jews (especially in 1881–83 and 1903–06). By the early twentieth century, about 4.5 million Jews had emigrated from the Russian Empire to North America; few ever return-migrated.

Czars, from 1648 until the fall of the dynasty in 1917, forced the migration to Siberia of hundreds of thousands of Russians convicted of political and other crimes. After 1861, however, the czars emancipated the serfs, enabling them to emigrate to Russian frontiers and cities or beyond Russia. By the early twentieth century, five million Christian Russians and other eastern Europeans had emigrated to North America.

Under Catherine and her successors, Russia expanded across Asia, using civilian emigrants as well as armies to expand its empire. Through wars with the weakening Ottoman Empire, Catherine annexed Crimea in 1783 (these empires warred again from 1853 to 1856 and 1877 to 1878). Eventually, Russian imperial armies, supported by about ten million Slavic settlers, extended Russian rule over various Muslim khanates east of the Caspian Sea, across Central Asia to the Pacific, and against the Qing Chinese Empire into the lands surrounding Manchuria.

Muslims living in lands annexed by Russia sometimes received generally tolerant treatment but were occasionally pressured to convert to Russian Orthodox Christianity. The Russian state considered nomadic Muslim communities especially dangerous; it therefore attempted to settle them as farmers, who were more easily taxed and controlled. Czars also deemed some Muslim and Christian communities in Crimea and the Caucasus disloyal and so expelled or resettled millions of them in less strategic places. Many Russians believed it their destiny to expand over all of Asia.

In 1891, the twenty-three-year-old imperial prince who would later become Czar Nicholas II (r. 1894–1917) and his staff traveled around Asia, examining European colonialism there and seeking ways to extend Russia's imperial borders. The final stage of the Trans-Siberian Railway, spanning the empire, had just been inaugurated. A leading imperial advisor, Prince Ukhtomskii, proclaimed that Russians by race and imperial right should lead all other Asians:

> Any Asiatic borderland soon becomes a home for a Russian. . . . In Asia we [Russians] have not, nor can have, any bounds, except the boundless sea breaking forever on her shores, an ocean as unfettered as is the spirit of the Russian people itself. . . . Our great golden-domed Moscow, which but a little earlier was no more than a small town in an insignificant subordinate principality, received the blessing of the saints and was irradiated by the creative glow of the autocratic idea. . . . [Now] the East . . . calls [Russians] onward to deeds of glory, to advancement beyond the bounds of a dull reality, to a bright, glorious, and ineffable future![17]

But, in 1904 and 1905, imperial Russia suffered major military defeats from a sometime ally but also rival power, Japan, which aspired to extend its own emigrants and imperial rule over East Asia and the Pacific.

In the mid-nineteenth century, Japan, which for two hundred years had officially banned immigration and emigration, suddenly emerged as a dynamic new empire. Internal pressures had been growing against the

*Many Japanese people found Commodore Matthew Perry and his 1853 and 1854 American naval and diplomatic missions alien, but they realistically recognized the unmatched power of his ships' guns. This popular print from that time, created by a Japanese artist, highlights Perry's absurd-looking face and clothing, showing both with a combination of American and Japanese features.* Courtesy Library of Congress Prints and Photographs Division, LC-USZC4-1307 shogun's Closed Country policy. When Commodore Matthew Perry brought American warships in 1853 and 1854 that threatened bombardment of Japan unless it opened to foreigners, many samurai mobilized to restore the emperor's rule.

Japan then reached out by sending official delegations of samurai to the United States (1860) and Europe (1862) and also selected students to move abroad for study. The Japanese Reformers' 1868 Charter Oath proclaimed: "Knowledge shall be sought throughout the world so as to strengthen the foundations of imperial rule."[18] The teenage, newly enthroned Emperor Meiji (r. 1867–1912) legitimated the Reformers' movement to transform Japan as they remodeled Japan's government, armed forces, schools, and economy, while striving to preserve what was best about Japan.

The 1890 Meiji Constitution freed peasants to emigrate from their hereditarily assigned lands, declaring that "Japanese subjects shall have the liberty of abode and of changing the same within the limits of law."[19] New transportation systems, including extensive railways, enhanced the movements of people and goods throughout Japan. New industries drew many workers to thriving cities and Japan mobilized virtually its entire population toward its new international ambitions.

Universal male conscription created national armed forces that extended Japan's empire across much of East Asia. In 1894 and 1895, Japanese armies defeated the weakening Qing Chinese Empire and seized Taiwan, which Japanese officials then went to administer. In 1900, the Japanese sent troops that—along with armies from Russia, the United States, and five European powers—crushed the massive Chinese Boxer Rebellion. This populist-nationalist uprising, mainly led by the Society of Righteous and Harmonious Fists, sought to expel all invasive foreigners and also Chinese Christian converts. Then, in 1904 and 1905, Japan's navy steamed to defeat decisively the Russian fleet, sent halfway around the world from its Baltic to its Pacific coast. Japanese soldiers and officials also went to rule Korea. Each expansion of Japanese forces across East Asia resulted in massive emigrations by local populations.

As the Japanese domestic population rose, the government began sponsoring emigration in 1885. Various Japanese commercial companies also recruited and sent out indentured and contract laborers. By 1900, about 65,000 Japanese emigrants had gone to Hawai'i; and by 1937, there were 200,000 Japanese in North America and 225,000 in Latin America. These emigrants and their children hereditarily retained their right to return to Japan as citizens, and many preserved cultural ties with their old homeland, even as they settled in their new one.

In 1934, twenty-one-year-old Mutsue Inomoto had an arranged marriage and immediately left her home in rural Japan to immigrate to Peru with her new thirty-seven-year-old husband, Naoichi Fujimori. Peru was the first of several Latin American countries to accept Japanese indentured laborers, starting in 1899, and would continue to do so until 1941. Her husband had already immigrated there as an indentured laborer in 1920, following two of his brothers. To encourage emigration, the Japanese government paid two-thirds of the passage money. However, her family struggled during Peru's political and economic turmoil. Many Spanish-speaking Peruvians were hostile to the small Japanese immigrant population in their midst. When her second child, Alberto, was born in 1938, they registered him at the Japanese consulate, thus officially giving him dual Japanese and Peruvian citizenship. He would grow up to be the controversial president of Peru (r. 1990–2000) who, after being convicted of human rights abuses and corruption, took refuge in Japan for years. His mother lived to see his rise and then imprisonment in Peru from 2007 onward.

Japan, China, Germany, India, and Israel, among other nations, follow the general principle of *jus sanguinis*, "right of blood." This means they accept as citizens or potential citizens all people who can demonstrate ancestry from their nation, including the foreign-born descendants of emigrants from their land, even several generations back. Conversely, however, this same principle makes it more difficult for people of a different ancestry to become citizens. Many Koreans who immigrated willingly or perforce to Japan have largely remained distinct from the rest of society. To different degrees, most nations regard ancestral ties to their dominant ethnicity as a major factor in eligibility for immigration and naturalization as a citizen.

In contrast, about 15 percent of nation-states, including the United States and France, have instead generally followed the birthright principle of *jus soli*, "right of soil," meaning anyone born of any ancestry within their national boundaries is a natural citizen. Nonetheless, not all people born in the United States or would-be immigrants have historically received the same treatment or status. At independence, the United States decided to include as its citizens all people born on its soil except slaves or Amerindians of sovereign tribes. Only in 1866 did the Constitution's Fourteenth Amendment recognize all people born on U.S. soil as citizens.

The leaders of the American Revolution were almost all immigrants or descendants of immigrants from Europe. U.S. policies have historically authorized the relatively easy naturalization of most types of immigrants; until 1820, the government did not even keep systematic records about who immigrated. Emma Lazarus's poem, written in 1883, which adorns the Statue of Liberty, "the Mother of Exiles," in New York harbor promises:

Give me your tired, your poor,
Your huddled masses yearning to breathe free,
The wretched refuse of your teeming shore,
Send these, the homeless, tempest-tossed to me,
I lift my lamp beside the golden door![20]

U.S. policies, however, have usually considered race, national origin, and physical and moral health as criteria in immigration or citizenship. The first Naturalization Act of 1790 declared that immigrants could only become citizens if they were residents for two years, were "free white persons," and were of "good moral character."[21]

All nations have at times discriminated among would-be immigrants and citizens. During the nineteenth and early twentieth centuries, the governments of Australia, Brazil, Canada, New Zealand, South Africa, and the United States, among others, advertised and gave financial subsidies for white European immigrants. But, at the same time, these governments made nonwhite people pay for their passage or enter indenture, and sometimes explicitly excluded some on racial grounds. Notably, after about 100,000 Chinese had immigrated to the United States, Congress passed the 1882 Chinese Exclusion Act that barred all "skilled and unskilled laborers and Chinese employed in mining" from entering the United States at all and also prohibited all Chinese not born on U.S. territory from ever becoming citizens (Congress only repealed this act in 1943).[22] All nations have continued to debate, and alter, policies about people entering or newly within their boundaries.

Wars often move national borders, making some settled people new citizens and others new aliens in the land where they have long lived. Following the Russo-Turkish War (1877–78), diplomatic negotiations called the Congress of Berlin reallocated territories from the Ottoman Empire to the Russian, Austro-Hungarian, and British empires and also created new countries. The diverse communities living in these various lands suddenly had to either accept their new status as subjects of a different ruler or emigrate.

Africa's interior had largely remained out of European colonial control due to endemic diseases like malaria and sleeping sickness (*trypanosomiasis*). But, in the late nineteenth century, new medicines, like the industrialization of quinine production for use against malaria, enabled

Europeans to immigrate and exploit sub-Saharan Africa's valuable minerals and other raw materials. This led to the "scramble" among European colonial powers, which their diplomats, meeting in the 1884 to 1885 Congress of Berlin, sought to regulate. These Europeans divided Africa, allotting the 80 percent of that continent not yet under colonial rule to various European states—if they sent settlers, officials, or soldiers there. Overall, the only African lands not under European colonial rule were Liberia and Ethiopia (which resisted one Italian invasion from 1889 to 1896 but later succumbed to another Italian invasion from 1935 to 1936). Indeed, with only a few exceptions, the entire world was divided between colonizing countries and their colonies. These new imperial-imposed borders around the world divided communities and displaced many people, even as governments enhanced the technology to regulate migrations.

Increasingly, governments set policies about who could cross their borders, and growing numbers of immigration agents enforced them. Many industrialists demanded cheap and docile laborers; therefore they and their governments sought to entice immigrants of ethnicities with this stereotype. Governments also developed their administrative capacity to identify and regulate the lives of people living within their borders. Official censuses since the mid-nineteenth century had become increasingly specific about the place of birth as well as age, race, and sex of every person living in every house in the country. Thus, international and intranational migrations had both been transformed by 1914 and would continue to be transformed over the next hundred years to the present.

## CHAPTER 5

# Migrations in an Age of Globalization, 1914 to the Present

Charles N'Tchoréré migrated from his African home in colonial Gabon to fight in France during both world wars (1914–18 and 1939–45). Indeed, about five million colonized subjects fought on behalf of their European rulers during these wars, while even more served as laborers attached to these armies. Their diverse experiences of migration beyond their homelands to European Asian or African battlefields changed their lives and their communities.

N'Tchoréré's ancestors, the Mpongwe, had settled in Gabon, coastal west Africa, around the sixteenth century as part of the larger Bantu migrations. Some Mpongwe then rose in prosperity and prominence as intermediary traders and slave suppliers for Europeans, who arrived in Gabon about the same time. Under French rule from 1885, his community became part of the colony's urbanized African elite, with loyal service to France and adoption of French language and culture as their prime path to advancement.

Charles N'Tchoréré was educated in the private, French Catholic–run École Montfort in his hometown of Libreville, Gabon. There, his teachers, who included French immigrants, used imported textbooks to instruct him about the glories of French culture and his privilege to aspire to share in it. But, in 1912 at age sixteen, he migrated with his businessman father 250 miles north to Cameroon, where he experienced a harsher regime under German colonizers. Later, he returned to Gabon to serve the French colonial administration.

At the outbreak of World War I, he enlisted at age twenty in the French colonial army. The French Army was still largely segregated by race, with separate African regiments known as the *Tirailleurs Sénégalais* (meaning skirmishers, or light infantry, from Senegal; Africans of all

JOURNÉE DE L'ARMÉE D'AFRIQUE
ET DES TROUPES COLONIALES

DEVAMBEZ . PARIS

This popular patriotic French poster portrays a tattered but undaunted soldier in the African Tirailleurs Sénégalais *(Senegalese Light Infantry)* charging over barbed wire into German trenches in France during World War I, followed *(from left to right)* by Asian Indo-Chinese, white French, and black African colonial soldiers. This 1917 poster symbolically projects hope, since the shattered tree still flowers over these men who have come from the colonies to save France. Poster by Lucien Jonas, courtesy Library of Congress Prints and Photographs Division, LC-USZC2-3949

ethnicities were labeled as Senegalese). He and his fellow African soldiers went to France and fought in the trenches against the Germans.
There, his exemplary conduct earned him promotion to sergeant. But,
like millions of other nonwhite colonial subjects who either willingly or
perforce served their European colonial rulers, he faced racial discrimi-
nation—not only from the German enemy but also from many white
French, British, and American soldiers and civilians.

After World War I, N'Tchoréré was one of the first Africans to earn
an officer's commission. His subsequent military career moved him
among several French colonies, including Sudan (now Mali) and Senegal, where he commanded the military academy for elite African youths
(this school was later renamed in his honor). Such circular migrations
from garrison to garrison were characteristic of many of the men and
women in the armed forces of any nation. After twenty years' service to
France, he retired in 1936, still only a lieutenant.

When World War II erupted and France again needed the aid of its
colonized subjects, N'Tchoréré left retirement to lead a battalion of Gab-
onese volunteer soldiers to France. There, he rose to the rank of captain
and command over African and white French infantry, making him one
of the first Africans whom France allowed to command white soldiers.
His son, Jean-Baptiste, also enlisted and came to fight in France as a cor-
poral. Showing their identification with their colonizer, his son wrote:
"Whatever happens papa, I will always be ready to defend our dear
country France."[1] His father replied how "proud" this loyalty made him.

As invading German tanks rolled over French defenders everywhere, Captain N'Tchoréré's unit suffered severe losses in June 1940.
He and the few survivors were forced to surrender. But his German
captors did not accept him as a gentleman officer and executed him for
refusing to leave the white French officers and join the African enlisted
men. His son died in combat soon thereafter. France honored his loyalty
by naturalizing him as a French citizen in 1940; Gabon, two years after
independence, issued a postage stamp in his honor in 1962 and erected
a statue of him in the capital. Like N'Tchoréré, people all over the earth
were displaced directly or indirectly by these two world wars.

Approximately 170 million men and women from most of the
world's countries and colonies left their homes to serve in uniform during
these world wars, often for years and on distant continents. Much of the
peaceful civilian intercontinental migration halted during each of these
wars. But the new military technologies of mechanized warfare, including
aerial attack with nuclear bombs, meant that invading and retreating
armies destroyed entire cities and drove out countless millions of civilians across continental Europe and much of Asia and Africa.

Following each war, victorious governments redrew many national boundaries and reallocated the losers' colonies. Some ethnic communities had their long-suppressed national aspirations for self-determination fulfilled, or partly fulfilled, by gaining their own country, either in the region where they were living currently or in a place to which they could emigrate. However, many other people found themselves and their long-established homes and communities under an alien government and among a different ethnic majority that considered them foreigners, often creating vast numbers of internally displaced persons (IDPs) and international refugees. For example, after each world war, the Balkans had many national borders moved or created that cut across its many ethnic groups.

During World War I and its aftermath, the losing German Hohenzollern, Austro-Hungarian Habsburg, and Turkish Ottoman multiethnic empires shattered as insurgent groups and the victorious allied powers broke them apart on the basis of national self-determination. The German Empire was largely replaced by a German Republic, but victorious European neighbors annexed several borderlands, driving many ethnic Germans to emigrate. France, Britain, Japan, Belgium, New Zealand, Australia, and Portugal forcibly took over German colonies in Africa and Asia. The Habsburg Empire eventually dissolved into Austria, Hungary, Poland, and Yugoslavia, with other territories distributed to other nations. The Ottoman Empire had long been fragmenting, as rival European empires and kingdoms seized its territories and dissident ethnic groups broke away. After World War I, the new Turkish Republic emerged in the Ottoman heartland while France imposed its mandate over Syria and Britain over Iraq, Transjordan, and Palestine. All these changes in government led to many emigrations and immigrations.

World War I also precipitated the 1917 revolution that broke apart the Russian Romanov Empire. This led to a vast civil war that displaced people across eastern Europe and much of Central Asia. The fighting only ended around 1922 with the creation of the Union of Soviet Socialist Republics (USSR) under Russian leadership, which eventually incorporated fifteen ethnically based national republics.

Joseph Stalin had immigrated from Georgia to Moscow and then seven times escaped from exile in Siberia. Rising with the Russian Communist revolution, he consolidated his totalitarian power over the USSR by 1924 and in subsequent decades imposed policies that dislocated virtually all its inhabitants. Farmland collectivization and rapid industrialization led many millions to leave the countryside for cities. His regime forced the migration to Siberia and Central Asia of about seven million people, sometimes by entire non-Russian ethnicities, including

Germans in the Volga region, Tatars in the Crimea, and various communities in the north Caucasus. In addition, Stalin ordered millions of alleged dissidents and rich peasant kulaks executed or shipped to forced labor camps, called the Gulag, spread across the USSR.

Following a global depression that made millions homeless, and then the Spanish Civil War (1936–39) that killed about 500,000 people and created as many refugees, the world mobilized again during World War II. The massive armies of the German Nazi regime and its Italian fascist ally conquered most of continental Europe while Japanese imperial forces expanded over much of East and Southeast Asia. Even larger numbers of Allied forces moved globally to oppose the Axis powers. The warring nations transported millions of captured soldiers to prisoner-of-war camps. During this total war, invading or retreating armies forced many millions of civilians to migrate by destroying their cities, towns, and villages. World War II made refugees of more than ninety million civilians in China, thirty-one million in Europe, and thirteen million in Japan.

*Japanese Americans board a train in Los Angeles bound for the War Relocation Camp at Manzanar in eastern California in April 1942. When the United States declared war on Japan following Japan's attack on Pearl Harbor on December 7, 1941, President Franklin Roosevelt issued Executive Order 9066, allowing the U.S. Army to intern more than 110,000 Japanese immigrants and their children living on the West Coast, about 60 percent of them U.S. citizens.* Photo by Russell Lee for the United States Farm Security Administration, courtesy Library of Congress Prints and Photographs Division, LC-USF33-013285-M1

Further, many belligerent governments imprisoned immigrants as alleged threats to national security. The Japanese incarcerated about 130,000 captured civilians, mostly Europeans, Australians, New Zealanders, and Americans; many suffered forced marches for long distances under deadly conditions. The United States shipped into isolated internment camps more than 110,000 American citizens and permanent residents of Japanese ancestry living on the West Coast. Other nations also rounded up residents of foreign ancestry or citizenship, no matter how innocent.

Karl Muffler apprenticed until age seventeen as a confectioner and pastry chef in Germany. He then practiced his profession for fifteen years, moving around Germany and then on a Spanish passenger ship. In 1930, an earlier German-Austrian immigrant to Melbourne, Australia, sponsored him as an employee. After four years in Melbourne, Muffler opened his own pastry shop, the Embassy, and married another German immigrant, Hilde Mayer. During World War II, however, the Australian government interned Muffler in a remote camp for six years as an enemy alien—like 12,000 other immigrants to Australia from thirty nations. Hilde was confined to a restricted area in Melbourne—like many other immigrant women and their children. After the war, Karl and Hilde were reunited and he resumed his cake-decorating career. They naturalized as Australian citizens in 1947, remaining the same people but transforming their legal national identity.[2]

During World War II, imperial Japanese forces invaded much of East and Southeast Asia, violently dislodging many civilians and often conscripting them for forced labor. About four million people in Indonesia alone died during the Japanese occupation. The Japanese also conscripted about 5.4 million Koreans as forced laborers and imported about 670,000 Koreans to Japan, while twice that number immigrated voluntarily seeking work. Following World War II, about 1.3 million Koreans repatriated but about 650,000 decided to remain in Japan, although as a minority community without citizenship (today, seventy years later, they number nearly a million, but most still are not Japanese citizens).

Especially brutal, the Nazi regime and its allies systematically concentrated in camps for slave labor or extermination specific groups, especially Jews, Roma, and Slavs, as well as others they declared undesirable, including communists and homosexuals. About six million of these people starved or died in poison gas chambers. To describe this brutal method of extermination, in 1948 the United Nations (UN) defined a new term, *genocide*, as "acts committed with intent to destroy, in whole or in part, a national, ethnical, racial or religious group."[3]

Subsequently, various other communities have described what their own people had suffered as genocide, including Armenians—more than a million of whom had long lived within the Ottoman Empire but died or fled in 1915. More recently, during a 1994 genocide in Rwanda, many of the majority Hutu killed about 800,000 of their minority Tutsi (and some Hutu) fellow citizens; when Tutsi military forces successfully invaded, about two million Hutu fled the country as international refugees. Currently, the International Criminal Court has indicted Sudan's president, General Omar al-Bashir (who took over in a 1993 coup), for genocide in its western province of Darfur, where about 500,000 non-Arab people have died and about 2.8 million are currently refugees. The international community has collectively set standards for the treatment of emigrants, although these standards are not always respected.

The two world wars affected millions, even people living in regions far from the fighting. During both wars, the disruption of civilian trans-Atlantic immigration to the United States and the enlistment and export of huge numbers of young men as soldiers created industrial labor shortages, especially as factories maximized war production. Many African Americans in the South had rising aspirations. Transportation by rail and road made several migrations in a lifetime, or even in a year, easier and cheaper. Thus, about six million African Americans migrated from the South to northern industrializing cities. Advocates of African American advancement, like the Chicago League on Urban Conditions among the [African American] Race, and eager employers encouraged these immigrants. Their migrations concentrated in two broad periods: during the world wars and the boom that followed each war, separated by a decline in migration during the Great Depression of the 1930s.

Some African Americans moved to join relatives or friends who had preceded them but others without connections applied for jobs long-distance. One African American woman in New Orleans replied in 1917 to an appeal in *The Defender*, an African American–owned Chicago newspaper and advocate of "The Great Migration Movement":

> Gentlemen: I read Defender every week and see so much good you're doing for the southern people & would like to know if you do the same for me as I am thinking of coming to Chicago about the first of June and wants a position. I have very fine references if needed. I am a widow of 28. No children, not a relative living and I can do first class work as house maid and dining room or care for invalid ladies. I am honest and neat and refined with a fairly good education. I would like a position where I could live on places because its very trying for a good girl to be out in a large city by self among strangers is why I would like a good home with good people. Trusting to hear from you.[4]

In recent decades, however, substantial numbers of African Americans have return-migrated to southern cities because some northern heavy industries have faltered while the South has developed and integrated as part of the economic world system.

In Asia and Africa, nationalist movements and the disruptions of World War II broke apart the British, French, Dutch, Japanese, and other colonial empires, thus creating new voluntary and forced migrations. Colonial boundaries had often cut across ethnic lines and also lumped together various diverse communities into single colonies. Hence, when these colonies became independent new nations, they included people who felt themselves an alienated minority. In Burma, Fiji, Sri Lanka, Uganda, Zanzibar, Zimbabwe, and many other new nations, politicians from the dominant ethnicity forced the brutal and sudden deportation or extermination of long-domiciled minority communities.

Nigeria, the most populous colony in Africa, was a British amalgamation of more than 250 ethnic communities speaking more than 500 languages. After independence in 1960, various groups vied for power over the whole nation, with the majority ethnicity in a region sometimes forcing long-settled minorities to emigrate. In 1967, the Igbo-dominated region in Nigeria's southeast seceded as its own nation, Biafra. This led to a bloody three-year civil war that dislocated most of the thirteen million Igbos living in Biafra or elsewhere in Nigeria and left a million dead. Finally, the invading Nigerian national army forced Igbos to accept political integration. Thus, the creation of any new nation leads to the fulfillment of the aspirations of some people but the alienation, and often emigration, of others.

Even before World War II, Indonesian nationalists struggled to create a new sense of unity among the diverse communities living on its more than 17,500 culturally distinct islands. After Japanese armies evacuated in 1945, the Netherlands imported 150,000 Dutch soldiers to restore its colonial rule, but widespread Indonesian opposition expelled them, and achieved independence in 1949. However, believing themselves alien minorities in the new nation, about 100,000 ethnic Chinese and about 40,000 Europeans who had long settled in Indonesia on-migrated to more welcoming nations or return-migrated to their ancestral lands. Many other anticolonial nationalists also mobilized their divided peoples against outsiders.

"I want to see the world," explained a twenty-one-year-old Vietnamese leaving Saigon in 1911 as a cook's assistant on a French steamship. During his lifetime, he used some fifty different names, largely to escape French surveillance, becoming most well-known under the alias Ho Chi Minh. Like many, he emigrated because he was dissatisfied with conditions in his colonized homeland and with aspirations for himself and his nation. Already, since age five, he had frequently migrated between his original village and Vietnam's historic imperial city, Hué, and he retained his rural accent throughout his tempestuous life. As his voyages took him across the Indian, Mediterranean, Atlantic, and Pacific oceans, he recalled that he "was observant of everything. Every time the boat was in the port, he did his utmost to visit the town. When he came back, his pocket was full of photos and matchboxes, for he liked to collect these things."[5]

Over the next dozen years, he labored aboard ships and in kitchens and workshops in New York, Boston, London, and Paris. But his life differed from most other emigrants because he had left colonial Vietnam to evade French police due to his youthful political activities. In Paris, Moscow, and then China, he became ever more committed to Vietnamese national independence and to communism as the best means of liberation. However, he did not revisit Vietnam for thirty years, when he return-migrated in 1941 to lead the independence revolution in the north that helped expel the Japanese in 1945 and drove out the French in 1954, but left South Vietnam under a separate government.

After this partition into communist North and capitalist South Vietnam, more than one million Vietnamese migrated between them, mostly Catholics moving to South Vietnam. Subsequently, each government drove many people from their homes for allegedly supporting the other. After warfare intensified, the United States intervened with combat troops in 1965 to defend South Vietnam's government. At the war's peak, 500,000 American and allied troops served there. North Vietnam finally reunited the nation in 1975, six years after Ho Chi Minh's death. Then, the communist regime moved two million alleged supporters of the former South Vietnamese government into reeducation camps. Additionally, over one million people fled the new regime.

Vietnam's wars also extended throughout former French colonial Indochina, creating refugees in neighboring Cambodia and Laos, including large numbers of ethnic minorities like the Hmong, whose mountainous homeland extended across several national boundaries. Many refugees were officially stateless emigrants, without any legal nationality. Large numbers sailed as vulnerable "boat people" through pirate-infested seas to any port that would receive them. The United States eventually accepted 823,000 of these refugees as legal immigrants.

In 1978, Vietnamese troops invaded Cambodia to depose Cambodia's Pol Pot regime, which had executed some two million fellow Cambodians. In retaliation, China invaded Vietnam in 1979 in a brief war involving 500,000 troops that dislocated millions in Vietnam's northern region. Subsequently, Vietnam's economic liberalization and integration into the global economy led to the migration by about one-third of the population to cities, spread some prosperity, and achieved entry into the World Trade Organization (WTO) in 2007.

After World War II, the victorious Allied powers ended Japan's colonial rule over Korea, and then divided it into North Korea and South Korea. Some 400,000 North Koreans migrated south, eventually followed by the huge communist North Korean army. In the war that ensued (1950–53), about 2.5 million Korean, Chinese, and UN soldiers (the latter mostly U.S. troops) moved up and down the peninsula, displacing almost all Koreans. Ever since, North Korea has sought isolation by preventing both emigration and immigration. In contrast, most other nations have substantial immigrant populations and also send out emigrants.

In 1947, the departing British partitioned their largest colony into the new nations of Pakistan and India on the basis of religious identity. At least twelve million people emigrated: Muslims moved to Islamic West or East Pakistan; Hindus and Sikhs to secular India. Up to two million emigrants died en route, and subsequent violent communal conflicts have continued to displace people throughout South Asia.

In 1971, the West Pakistani–dominated army devastated secessionist East Pakistan, displacing many of the seventy million Bengalis and driving about ten million refugees into neighboring India. Many returned as freedom fighters for their new nation, Bangladesh. Subsequently, at least four million Bangladeshi citizens, largely seeking economic advancement, have emigrated to India, often illegally. Indeed, in recent decades, within all the new nations of South Asia, hundreds of millions of people have migrated either internally from rural to urban areas or internationally.

Currently, the UN estimates 214 million people live outside of the country of their birth. Australia and Switzerland have more than a quarter of their populations born abroad. Almost a quarter of all people in the United States are international immigrants or the children of immigrants. But many people serial or on-migrate; about one in five legal immigrants into the United States in 2000 had then emigrated out by 2005. A few nations consist mostly of recent immigrants.

In Israel, most of the 5.7 million Jewish citizens (or their parents) are recent immigrants. In 1948, the British mandate over Palestine ended when the UN created the state of Israel as a national homeland for globally dispersed Jews. The new Israeli government soon passed its Law of Return, authorizing immigration by all Jews (extended in 1970 to people not religiously Jewish but who have Jewish grandparents or spouses). Further, the current Israeli government encourages Jewish immigration to settlements in the West Bank and east Jerusalem. But many of the 1.8 million Muslim and Christian citizens of Israel feel themselves alienated minorities in their ancestral and holy land.

Palestinians experienced the creation of Israel as a disaster, or *Nakba*, in Arabic. In 1949, the UN created the United Nations Relief and Works Agency (UNRWA) to provide governmental and public services for these Palestinian refugees in Jordan, Lebanon, and Syria, and in Israeli-controlled territory, who lacked their own internationally recognized state. Israel's expansion following the 1967 war added to their number, which totals about five million today. Other post–World War II international organizations also seek to manage international migrants.

In place of their empires, the British and French each created an association of their former colonies, which fostered migration among them. Due to labor shortages following World War II, Britain's 1948 Nationality Act allowed any of the 800 million citizens of the Commonwealth or its remaining empire to immigrate to Britain. However, since the 1960s after 1.5 million nonwhite immigrants had settled in Britain, that government instituted various restrictive immigration policies. Britain still debates whether to assimilate its nonwhite citizens into a unified British culture or to preserve their diversity within a multicultural Britain. Similarly, many societies debate making themselves either "melting pots," where all immigrants blend into one culture speaking one official language, or "salad bowls," where diversity is preserved in a "tasteful" mix.

Many long-settled white people return-migrated to their ancestral homes from newly liberated French, British, and other European colonies in Asia, Africa, and the Caribbean. After Algeria achieved independence in 1962, about 800,000 white French colonizers, self-described *Pieds-Noirs* (Black Feet), emigrated to mainland France, while about 200,000 chose to remain in Algeria as an ethnic minority. After Zimbabwe achieved independence in 1980 and South Africa ended apartheid in 1993, many whites emigrated to Britain, Australia, Canada, or other predominantly white Commonwealth dominions. About 100,000 Europeans left the Congo in 1960 when Belgian colonial rule ended. As these immigrants resettled in the land their ancestors had left, many campaigned against allowing immigration by other ethnicities.

While each nation sets its own immigration goals and policies, most have recognized the need for uniform international migration standards that respect both national and human rights. The League of Nations (1920–46) and then the UN (1945 onward) have been the most prominent multinational bodies seeking to regulate international immigration.

Following the massive legal, illegal, and undocumented migrations caused by World War I, the League of Nations in 1920 convened the International Conference on Passports and Customs Formalities and Through Tickets that established the current system of standardized passports, visas, and other official travel documents. The goal was definitively to identify all people individually as they migrated internationally—although this has not yet been fully implemented nearly a century later.

In 1930, the League of Nations' Hague Convention promised that "every person should have a nationality," but more than twelve million "stateless" people today do not have one.[6] Political boundaries still divide the Kurds, twenty million of whom today live as alienated minorities within Iraq, Turkey, Iran, and Syria. Further, the League asserted that "every person . . . should have one nationality only." Yet, almost half the world's governments recognize dual nationality in some form—often naturalized immigrants are allowed to retain citizenship in the nation of their birth.

In 1948, the UN passed the Universal Declaration of Human Rights that promises: "Everyone has the right to freedom of movement and residence within the borders of each State [and] has the right to leave any country, including his own, and to return to his country."[7] This does not, however, promise free entry into another country. Rather, each nation retains the right to regulate immigration of noncitizens; these policies vary widely.

The Cold War that followed World War II divided the world into three spheres: the First World of Western nations and their allies; the Third World of nonaligned nations; and the Second World of the USSR and its allies, behind what Winston Churchill popularized as the Iron Curtain. Most, but not always all, nations in the First and Third Worlds have respected the Universal Declaration's pledge of free movement of citizens within their borders, unconstrained emigration, and the right of reentry for its citizens. But totalitarian states, especially within the Soviet Bloc, tried to control both migration within their borders as well as emigration across them.

In 1961, after 2.5 million Germans moved from East to West Germany, along with other large-scale emigrations from the Soviet Bloc, East Germany built the Berlin Wall dividing that city, as part of an extensively patrolled border separating Soviet citizens from western Europe. Only after eastern Europeans demolished this wall in 1989 did they regain the ability to emigrate. Less than a year later, West and East Germany reunited and accepted about two million ethnic German immigrants from eastern Europe.

*Many people died trying to emigrate from eastern to western Europe during the Cold War. This 1990 photograph shows a long row of crosses commemorating men and women who died trying to escape the Soviet Bloc through the Berlin Wall; the graffiti shows West Berliners' disrespect for this barrier to migration.* Courtesy U.S. Department of Defense, VIRIN DF-ST-92-00211

The Cold War ended in 1991, when the USSR dissolved into its fifteen ethnically based national republics, largely restoring national self-determination to the majority community within each. But millions of ethnic Russians who had settled in those lands suddenly found themselves a disempowered minority; 5.4 million of them return-migrated to Russia. Further, uneven economic development within the nations of the former USSR have led nearly seven million non-Russian people to immigrate into Russia, only about 2.8 million of them legally. Popular Russian hostility against non-Russian immigrants, many of them Muslims, has been rising in response.

Even more violently, Yugoslavia shattered amid brutal fighting among its many ethnic groups (1991–2003). Forced expulsions and massacres of minority communities have created separate ethnic-based nations—Bosnia and Herzegovina, Croatia, Kosovo, Macedonia, Montenegro, Serbia, and Slovenia—as well as Vojvodina as an autonomous province within Serbia. This violence also produced the term *ethnic cleansing*: the rendering of an area ethnically homogeneous by using force or intimidation to remove persons of another ethnic or religious group. But the practice of expelling minorities, which often overlaps with genocide, has a long and violent history. Ethnicity, however, is only one basis for large-scale migrations.

Over the past two hundred years in China, economic forces, wars, and government policies have attracted or compelled growing numbers of migrants. Between 1850 and World War II, new transportation links opened Manchuria as a farming frontier, which attracted thirty million people from China to push northeast beyond the Great Wall; about one-third of them settled there permanently (additionally, about ten million Russians, two million Koreans, and 500,000 Japanese also emigrated to Manchuria). When the Qing Empire fell in the 1911 revolution, China fragmented into disorder and mass dislocation.

Dr. Sun Yat-sen, a man who had spent much of his life overseas, returned as the new Chinese Republic's president (1911–13). He had been educated in Hawai'i (and, at times, claimed to have been born there) and had often lived as part of the large trans-Pacific Chinese diaspora community; today, this includes 35 million ethnic Chinese people. But long after Sun's death in 1925, forced migrations continued to plague China, in large part due to contending Chinese warlords, political parties, the Japanese invasion, and World War II.

During this multisided fighting, 100,000 Chinese Communist Party (CCP) emigrants made the Long March, lasting more than a year (1934–35) and covering hundreds of miles from southeast and central China to Yunan in the northwest. This migration bound the relatively few survivors into a powerful CCP cadre. By 1949, the CCP had mobilized peasants and armies, driving its enemies from mainland China, including about two million anticommunist Chinese who migrated to Taiwan. Further, claiming to restore China's historic borders, Chinese armies entered Tibet in 1950, followed by many Han Chinese settlers, leading more than 100,000 Tibetans, led by the Dalai Lama, to flee into exile in India and elsewhere.

The CCP's policies have displaced many. Land collectivization dislocated tens of millions and the ill-planned economic transformation called the Great Leap Forward (1958–61) another sixty million. The Cultural Revolution (1966–76) mobilized millions of ardent youth into the Red Guards, who moved throughout China expelling alleged class enemies. They forced tens of millions, including eighteen million students or recent graduates, to move from cities to rural areas for years of reeducation. The opening of China's economy, especially since 2000, has led to the largest peacetime migration in world history, despite official prohibition of internal migration.

At present, China has about 260 million people living away from their official home, including about 160 million long-term rural-to-urban migrants. Yet, the People's Republic of China (PRC), under its *Hukou* system, requires everyone to be officially registered in one locality and to not emigrate without special permission. At various times, other governments, including in Japan, North and South Korea, and Vietnam, have imposed similar registration systems. But the PRC makes it especially difficult for people to change their registration, especially from rural to urban localities. Nonetheless, China's widespread economic reforms at the start of this century have led to massive migrations to cities, especially to export-oriented factories along the coast. For the first time in history, more than half of China's population (currently 1.35 billion) lives in cities; one hundred years ago less than one-fourth did so. But the Hukou system has kept rural registrants and their children—even if they are longtime residents or were born in a city—unable to settle legally, attend state schools, or receive other government benefits. Their unregistered status also depresses their wages, although usually at levels higher than in their legal rural residences.

In 2000, seventeen-year-old Wang Cuihua emigrated more than six hundred miles from his village in Shandong Province to Anshan, a steel-manufacturing industrial and commercial city. There, he found work in restaurant kitchens. As he told a fellow worker (who was also an English anthropologist):

> I'm not scared of you laughing, when I first came out from the countryside I didn't even know that I should wash my feet before I slept; I only washed them once a week. This was really dirty. Later, slowly, after a year, I realized that other people washed them every day, and so I tried it a couple of times. Ah! My feet felt so comfortable! After this I slowly began to change in other ways too. . . . I used to only require that clothing was warm in the cold, but now I also want it to look good. Perhaps in another few years my requirements will change again, so that not only is it good-looking but that I also pursue the latest trends. That'd be even better.

Wang secretly studied via the Internet to improve his sophistication and success. His favorite book is the biography of Sir Li Jiacheng, a refugee from mainland China to Hong Kong who worked his way up from factory floor to become one of the world's richest Asians. Wang explained, "I read and apply what I learn to my life. . . . I don't want to be mediocre; I don't want an ordinary life. If this year I don't have enough money to realize my dreams I'll just keep working on for another half year, a full year." Gradually, setting and meeting self-imposed goals,

Wang accumulated experience and seniority until he became the restaurant's kitchen supervisor, earning double the wage of new arrivals from villages.[8]

Wang also incrementally improved his living conditions, acquiring the best room in his dormitory, which he decorated with fish and plants, and only shared with one other person, a more recent immigrant and his junior "apprentice." He found city life altogether more "civilized": "How can I say? In every respect . . . the city is cleaner than the countryside. The conditions in the village are not good. . . . There are no leisure places, karaoke and discos in the village."[9] However, unable to change his official registration to this city, he remained part of China's huge "floating population" without legal rights or access to government health care or other services.

After what was supposed to be a brief trip home to see his family, Wang stayed in his village to marry. He will perhaps emigrate to a city again in the future. Typically, enterprising young Chinese rural men and women have periodically emigrated to cities, returned home to wed, then again emigrated, entrusting their children to elderly relatives until they themselves reach middle or old age and remain in the village. But recently the pace of rural-to-urban migration has slowed as China's underemployed labor pool is diminished and as rural development and wages rise. China is also slowly becoming an international immigration destination.

In 1949, the CCP deported most of the 200,000 foreigners then living in China and then, for decades, the PRC discouraged immigration. But now a growing number of foreigners are seeking work in China, especially Koreans, Burmese, Vietnamese, Africans, and Russians. China's 2010 census identified 1,020,145 foreigners living in the PRC (40 percent of them citizens of Taiwan or Hong Kong). Further, China's longstanding "One Child Policy" has led many families to choose to keep only a son, thus creating a substantial shortage of women, less than 8.5 for every 10 men. Consequently, a small but rising number of Chinese men are importing brides from elsewhere in Asia. Additionally, one million Chinese students and scholars have studied abroad since 1996; more than a quarter, dubbed "sea turtles," have already re-immigrated to China. Most immigrants have faced legal and cultural difficulties settling in China. But China's aging population means it will depend increasingly on immigrant workers. Further, the WTO, which China joined in 2001, and the UN require that legal immigrant workers receive equal treatment with citizens.

The nations of the UN are protective of their own sovereignty and resist outside interference within their borders. Except in extreme circumstances or when requested by the host, the UN does not intervene within a nation by asserting protection over IDPs. Rather, the UN generally only protects refugees who have crossed an international border for reasons it considers valid. The UN's 1951 Refugee Convention specifies that a legitimate refugee is someone who, "owing to a well-founded fear of being persecuted for reasons of race, religion, nationality, membership of a particular social group or political opinion, is outside the country of his nationality, and is unable to, or owing to such fear, is unwilling to avail himself of the protection of that country."[10] Economic migrants or violators of human rights or of criminal laws generally do not qualify.

The UN defines someone smuggled or trafficked across an international border as an "illegal immigrant" and someone without documentation or legal sanction as an "irregular immigrant." Both types are vulnerable to deportation or imprisonment by the host nation, although the Universal Declaration of Human Rights requires hosts to offer asylum to refugees who emigrated for legitimate reasons. About 500,000 refugees annually request asylum, but not all are successful.

In 1950, the UN created the office of High Commissioner for Refugees (UNHCR) to "lead and co-ordinate international action to protect refugees and resolve refugee problems worldwide . . . to safeguard the rights and well-being of refugees [and] to ensure that everyone can exercise the right to seek asylum and find safe refuge in another State, with the option to return home voluntarily, integrate locally or to resettle in a third country."[11] The UN estimates that there are currently more than 43 million forcibly displaced persons in the world, with events like the violence in Syria and Myanmar tragically adding to that number. Of these forced emigrants, about twelve million are "stateless" to whom the UNHCR can issue travel documents, called "Nansen passports" after the first commissioner for refugees, Fridtjof Nansen. When 25,000 or more refugees of the same nationality have been in a host country for five or more years, the UNHCR defines this as a "protracted refugee situation." Currently, more than seven million refugees in twenty-six host countries suffer this. The UNHCR seeks a durable solution for all refugees. Often, this means repatriation, which the UNHCR estimates 2.3 million refugees to have done over the past five years. Many of those refugees had been temporarily admitted as immigrant workers before they were expelled.

Various nations have allowed laborers to immigrate temporarily, without the right to naturalize. The United States had the *Bracero* (Strong-Arms) Program (1942–64) to import temporary workers from

Mexico. When Germany needed more laborers in the 1960s to 1970s, it allowed *Gastarbeiter* (guest workers), mainly Turks, to enter; there are currently about four million people of Turkish ancestry living in Germany, many without German citizenship. Currently, many oil-rich nations of the Persian Gulf have millions of temporary Asian laborers, including women servants, many from the Philippines, Nepal, or Bangladesh. They endure hardship and isolation, often in order to remit their earnings to their families back home. Globally, official remittances total more than $500 billion annually, mostly from immigrant workers in rich nations to their families in poor ones; in addition, hundreds of billions in remittances pass through unofficial money-transfer networks. Temporary workers are vulnerable to sudden deportation and their families, sometimes including citizens, also suffer disruption.

Late in Muammar Qaddafi's oil-rich regime (1969–2011), Hanif had left his home in Bangladesh to immigrate to Libya as a guest worker, without the right of permanent residence.[12] He was one of about two million other foreign workers in Libya, including 60,000 Bangladeshis, 30,000 Chinese, 30,000 Filipinos, 30,000 Tunisians, 23,000 Thai, 18,000 Indians, 10,000 Vietnamese, 10,000 Turks, 1,500,000 Egyptians, and uncounted thousands of sub-Saharan Africans. During the violence in Libya from the 2011 Arab Spring insurrection, richer governments evacuated their citizens, but poorer governments did not, causing about 180,000 people to flee to UNHCR refugee camps.

Simultaneously, the Bangladesh government leased thousands of soldiers or police to UN peacekeeping forces, many stationed in surrounding lands—Darfur, South Sudan, Western Sahara, Côte d'Ivoire, Liberia, Democratic Republic of the Congo, and Lebanon. In fact, Bangladesh has provided about 10 percent of the 100,000 personnel of UN peacekeeping forces around the world, having been posted to forty-seven separate conflict zones, more than any other nation. The UN pays Bangladesh for these men's services and, as UN peacekeepers stationed in distant lands, they receive better training and equipment than their own government provides. Other international organizations have also enabled new kinds of migrations, with Europe taking a leading role.

The foundational 1992 Maastricht Treaty of the European Union (EU) proclaims: "Every citizen of the Union shall have the right to move and reside freely within the territory of the Member States, subject to . . . limitations and conditions."[13] This created an international zone of free migration for almost all the 500 million citizens of its twenty-eight member nations.[14] But, as the EU has been admitting more nations, several older member-states have reserved their sovereign powers by imposing "limitations and conditions" on migrations from some newer member-states. France, among other nations, currently requires citizens of Romania and Bulgaria, which joined the EU in 2007, to obtain special permits in order to work in certain professions or remain more than three months.

Most, but not all, EU states (plus five others) signed the 1985 Schengen treaty, creating a zone within which all people can migrate freely without a passport or visa. This Schengen region of unconstrained migration includes the four hundred million citizens of the twenty-six signatory nations and also anyone else admitted at any border checkpoint. Hence, some current members object to inclusion into the Schengen area of some applicant nations, like Bulgaria and Romania, which they believe have insecure border controls.

Even though migrations across national borders within the EU or Schengen area have increased, levels of international migration still remain lower than migrations within any single nation, in Europe, and elsewhere. National boundaries still limit most migrations due to the

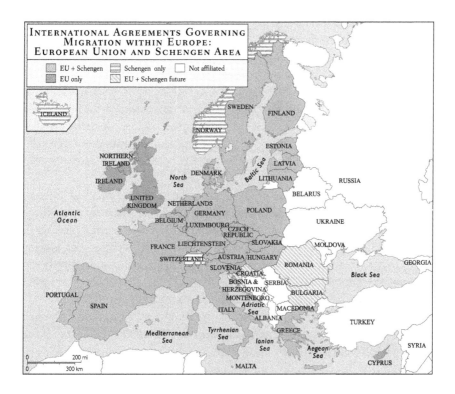

deeply felt sense of being part of a national imagined community, bound together by law, economics, historical origins, and culture. Adding barriers to immigration, many powerful (or aspirational) nativist or "sons of the soil" political parties and movements have arisen around the world, including within most EU and Schengen nations. Their adherents identify themselves exclusively with their land and express hostility and resentment against immigrants, particularly during times of economic stress and high unemployment. Some such groups explicitly deny that they were themselves ever immigrants, asserting rather that they are native to their homeland, which they will defend against immigrants. Yet, such claims suppress their own immigration histories.

Many of the often-discriminated-against Aborigines in Australia, Adivasis in India, Native Americans in the United States, First Nations in Canada, Amazonian communities in Brazil, and other "indigenous" people in almost every land assert that they were the original inhabitants, divinely created as humans on the spot where they currently live. Some then base claims on that religious assertion for recovery of their primal homeland or else compensation for displacement from it. Even among self-acknowledged immigrant communities, believing that one arrived in a place first remains a powerful self-justifying moral argument for possession of that place.

Maoris remember their twelfth- to fourteenth-century *heke* from Hawaiiki (perhaps Tahiti) into today's New Zealand. Many other cultures also commemorate their epic immigration, often with great hardship, as a baptismal "Great Migration" that has risen to sacred status. In many instances, however, this immigration displaced or subordinated people already living there. Thus, competing immigrants can have contradictory claims to the same land, reciprocally identifying each other as illegal intruders.

One of the controversial policies of former French president Nicolas Sarkozy (r. 2007–12) was the dismantling in 2010 of some three hundred illegal settlements in France, mostly inhabited by Roma from Romania or Bulgaria. His government deported or gave a cash payment for leaving voluntarily to nearly a thousand alleged itinerants, criminals, or simply undocumented people. Yet, Sarkozy was himself the son of an immigrant father and a maternal grandfather and he also married immigrants.

His father, Pál Sárközy, was born in Budapest, Hungary, and then fled the communist government there in 1945, at age seventeen, and joined the French Foreign Legion. After being stationed in Algeria, he obtained his discharge on medical grounds on the eve of his unit's departure to fight in French colonial Indochina. Then, for twenty-two years, he lived in France as a stateless person, although a legal resident, before gaining French citizenship in 1970. In 1949, he married Andrée Mallah; her father was a Jewish immigrant to France from Greece, who had legally settled in France and converted to Catholicism. Hence, their son, Nicolas, was born to a legally stateless father, although an increasingly wealthy one, and a mother who was an immigrant's daughter. Nicolas's second wife, Cecilia Attias, was also the daughter of immigrants: a Jewish Moldovan father and Spanish mother. Then, while president of France, Nicolas married his current wife, Carla Bruni, a fashion model-turned-singer who herself immigrated from Italy and has become a naturalized French citizen. Thus, some immigrants who can obtain legal status may safely prosper, but those without the correct cultural identity or documents or wealth are subject to deportation whenever a government decides to do so.

Throughout the past 200,000 years of Homo sapiens' history, we have migrated for diverse reasons. Current human migration patterns have both continuities with the past and also features distinctive to our

*The U.S. government has erected this extensive wall along much of its border with Mexico. Many nations have built similar barriers with the same goal of trying to prevent unauthorized immigration.* Photo courtesy Office of Representative Phil Gingrey, U.S. Congress, 2008

age. We have always immigrated seeking more, be it natural resources— including animals to hunt, fodder for herds, better farmland, or mineral wealth—or to improve our social, cultural, or economic condition. We have also often emigrated out of desperation or dissatisfaction with our current situation. Cultural factors like religion and political beliefs continue to motivate many to migrate. Personal factors like marriages and divorces have almost always resulted in migration. Clashes among individuals and groups have historically caused and resulted from migrations, as invading groups or armies create fleeing refugees who themselves then often cause secondary emigrations by people they encounter. Wars, ethnic tensions, and other conflicts still create millions of new refugees annually.

But there are now more than seven billion Homo sapiens moving over the earth. Our numbers have almost quadrupled over the last hundred years. The current populations of China (1.35 billion) and India (1.24 billion) together equal the entire world's population in 1950. Indeed, China today holds about the entire world population of 1910. This means that competing immigrant and settled communities often claim the same space. Life-long nomads and other herders have greatly diminished as a proportion of the human population as farming and then urban-based industries have attracted ever more immigrant settlers.

Our rapidly developing technologies have altered the speed, volume, and velocity of migrations. Our transportation systems enable almost all people to make rapid trans- or intercontinental migrations. The globalized economic system of production and consumption has led to emigration from poorer nations to richer ones through "brain drains" for educated people and "muscle drains" for manual laborers. Our vastly expanded energy extraction has enabled widespread industrialization and prosperity for many. Our ever more sophisticated means of food production, including the Green Revolution and genetic engineering of crops as well as industrialized fishing, and global food distribution networks have enabled more than half of the world's population to live in urban areas. This is far more in absolute numbers and also more as a proportion than ever before in history. Currently, extended Tokyo contains nearly thirty-seven million people, more than a quarter of Japan's national population. But the environmental changes humans have created are also now increasing the number of ecological refugees, including both those displaced directly from massive dams and other human constructions and also indirectly from global warming as deserts are spreading, sea levels are rising, and climate instability displaces ever more people annually.

Our national governments can also, in ever more extensive ways, track and manage our movements, both internally and internationally. Currently, the world's governments have moved about ten million people into prisons (about one quarter of these are in the United States alone) where their movements are fully controlled. Both border agents and police can use electronic records and biometrics to monitor people's international and intranational movements.

Migrations have deeply affected our identities, and museums, archives, and monuments throughout much of the world have attempted to reconstruct and commemorate them. Individuals use DNA tests, online records, and other sources to discover and trace their genealogies far back in history. Nongovernmental organizations and community-sponsored institutions often feature the migration history of their own particular ethnicity. Many government-funded projects include in their national narratives both immigrants and also the people left behind when others emigrated. Most such museums solicit contributions from visitors, not only financial but also by adding their own personal or family stories, papers, or artifacts to the collection. These efforts counteract anti-immigrant sentiments and also preserve a sense of how our societies were constituted. Such efforts resonate with our widespread fascination with where we came from, because we are all migrants and migration history is the core of world history.

# Chronology

CA. 200,000 BCE
Homo sapiens emerge in Africa as a physically distinct species

CA. 100,000 BCE
Homo sapiens in Africa develop language and other distinctive cultural features

CA. 70,000–60,000 BCE
Homo sapiens expand their range beyond Africa into Eurasia

CA. 20,000–15,000 BCE
Last major ice age; Homo sapiens expand their range into Australia and the Americas

CA. 12,000–1500 BCE
Various communities in Africa, Eurasia, and the Americas stop migrating and settle as farmers: Agricultural Revolution

CA. 8000 BCE–CA. 500 BCE
Indo-European migrations from Central Asia across southern and western Asia and Europe

CA. 3500–CA. 2700 BCE
Walled cities are first created in China, Mesopotamia, and along the Nile and the Indus rivers

CA. 3000 BCE–CA. 500 CE
Polynesians migrate to most islands in the Pacific

CA. 1050 BCE–CA. 600 BCE
Greek diaspora in Mediterranean and west Asia

CA. 300 CE–CA. 500 CE
Germanic migrations across Europe and north Africa

CA. 500–PRESENT
Roma migrations from India across west Asia, north Africa, and Europe

622–PRESENT
Expansion of Islam globally

CA. 790–CA. 1100
Scandinavian outward migrations in Atlantic world and eastern Europe

1095–CA. 1300
Roman Catholic Crusades from Europe to Levant

1206–CA. 1500
Mongol expansion, followed by empires across much of Eurasia

CA. 720–1492
Roman Catholic Reconquista of Iberia ending with expulsion of Jews and Muslims

1405–33
Voyages of Zheng He sponsored by Ming dynasty in China

1433–1893
Sea Ban edicts against immigration or emigration by several Chinese dynasties

1492 ONWARD
Spanish, Portuguese, and other European colonization of Americas, Africa, and Asia

CA. 1510–1815
European trans-Atlantic trade in enslaved Africans

1600–1868
Shogunate rule in Japan with Closed Country Edict (1635–ca. 1860)

1618–48
Thirty Years' War in Europe ending with Treaty of Westphalia (1648)

CA. 1620–CA. 1780
European indentured labor to Americas

1718–1868
British convicts transported to Americas, then Australia

**CA. 1740s–1902**
Afrikaner treks into inland south Africa, creating Transvaal and Orange Free State

**CA. 1750 ONWARD**
Industrial Revolution in western Europe, later developed in North America and then globally

**1787, 1792**
Sierra Leone established in west Africa for return-migrating people of African descent

**1789**
French Revolution followed by Napoleonic Wars (1799–1815)

**CA. 1820–CA. 1920**
Asian indentured labor migration system

**1821**
Liberia established by United States' Back to Africa Movement

**1830**
Indian Removal Act in United States

**1845–50**
Potato blight in western Europe followed by massive emigrations

**1884–85**
Congress of Berlin regularizes European Scramble to colonize Africa

**1914–18**
World War I

**1920–46**
League of Nations followed by United Nations (1945–present)

**1939–45**
World War II followed by independence for most former colonies of European and Japanese empires

**1945–91**
Cold War

**1950–PRESENT**
United Nations High Commissioner for Refugees

**1985–PRESENT**
Schengen treaty zone of free migration in Europe

**1992–PRESENT**
European Union formed from European Community

# Notes

**PREFACE**

1. Anonymous, "Vinland Sagas," trans. Keneva Kunz, in *Sagas of Icelanders: A Selection* (New York: Penguin, 2000), 644.

**CHAPTER 1**

1. South Tyrol Museum of Archaeology, accessed April 19, 2013, www.iceman.it.
2. *The Epic of Gilgamesh*, trans. Maureen Gallery Kovacs (Stanford: Stanford University Press, 1985), 3.
3. Ibid., 6.
4. Ibid., 4.
5. Autobiography of Weni, Cairo Museum No. 1435, Sixth Dynasty, in Miriam Lichtheim, *Ancient Egyptian Literature* (Berkeley: University of California Press, 1973), 1: 20–21.
6. Ibid.
7. Rig Veda 1.85.9, 1.32.11–12, trans. Wendy Doniger O'Flaherty, *The Rig Veda* (Harmondsworth: Penguin, 1981), 150, 166.
8. Diodorus Siculus, *History*, Loeb Classical Library (Cambridge: Harvard University Press, 1963), vol. 8, book 17, verse 2.
9. Ibid., book 94, verse 2.
10. Martial, *Epigrams*, IX.3, in William Stearns Davis, *Readings in Ancient History: Illustrative Extracts from the Sources* (Boston: Allyn and Bacon, 1913), 2: 225.
11. Ammianus Marcellinus, *Res Gestae*, in C. D. Yonge, *Roman History* (London: Bohn, 1862), 575–79.

**CHAPTER 2**

1. *Quran*, Sura 16, verse 41, trans. Saheeh International (London: Al-Muntada Al-Islami, 2004), 253.
2. Quoted in N. Levitzion and J. F. P. Hopkins, eds., *Corpus of Early Arabic Sources for West African History* (Cambridge: Cambridge University Press, 1981), 269–73.
3. Ibn Khaldun, *Muqaddimah: An Introduction to History*, trans. Franz Rosenthal, ed. N. J. Dawood (Princeton: Princeton University Press, 1967), 107, 264.
4. Nizam al-Mulk, *Book of Government, or Rules for Kings: The* Siyar al-muluk, *or* Siyasat-nama *of Nizam al-Mulk*, trans. Hubert Darke (London: Routledge and Kegan Paul, 1978), 117.
5. Ibn Battuta, *Travels of Ibn Battuta*, trans. H. A. R. Gibb (Cambridge: Hakluyt Society, 1958–71), 2: 282–83.
6. Ibid., 2: 235.
7. Quoted in Louise Levathes, *When China Ruled the Seas: The Treasure Fleet of the Dragon Throne, 1405–1433* (Oxford: Oxford University Press, 1996), 17.
8. Lady Sarashina, "Diary of Lady Sarashina (1009–1059)," trans. Annie Shepley Omori and Kochi Doi, in *Diaries of Court Ladies of Old Japan* (Boston: Houghton Mifflin, 1920), 3.
9. Ibid., 44.

10. Bouquet, *Recueil des Historiens des Gaules et de las France*, in *Source Book of Mediaeval History: Documents Illustrative of European Life and Institutions from the German Invasions to the Renaissance*, ed. Frederic Austin Ogg (New York: Cooper Square, 1972), 168.

11. Ibid.

12. Peter Heather, *Empires and Barbarians: The Fall of Rome and the Birth of Europe* (Oxford: Oxford University Press, 2010), 491ff.

13. Snorre Sturlason, *Heimskringla*, trans. Samuel Laing (London: Norroena Society, 1844), 3: 794.

14. Marco Polo, *Travels of Marco Polo*, trans. William Marsden, ed. Thomas Wright (London: Henry G. Bohn, 1854), 128.

15. Ibid., 122–23.

16. Ibid.

17. David Morgan, *Mongols* (Oxford: Blackwell, 2007), 74.

18. Yvo of Narbonne to Archbishop of Burdeaux, containing a confession of an Englishman, recorded by Matthew Paris, 1243, in Samuel Purchas, ed., *Hakluytlus Posthumus, or, Purchas his Pilgrimes* (Glasgow: Glasgow University Press, 1907), 11: 186–87.

19. Godfrey Rupert Carless Davis, *Magna Carta* (London: British Library, 1971), 21.

20. Quoted in R. H. C. Davis, *History of Medieval Europe: From Constantine to Saint Louis* (London: McKay, 1957), 373.

21. Ibid.

22. Annalist of Nieder-Altaich, *The Great German Pilgrimage of 1064–65*, trans. James A. Brundage, *The Crusades: A Documentary History* (Milwaukee, WI: Marquette University Press, 1962), 3–4.

23. Anna Comnena (Komnene), *The Alexiad*, trans. Elizabeth A. Dawes (London: Routledge, Kegan, Paul, 1928), 248–52.

24. Ibid.

25. Usama ibn Munqidh, *Autobiography*, trans. Franceso Gabrieli and E. J. Costello, *Arab Historians of the Crusades* (New York: Routledge, 2010), 44–50.

26. Ibid.

CHAPTER 3

1. Babur, Zahir al-Din, *Baburnama*, trans. Wheeler M. Thackston (New York: Modern Library, 2002), 171.

2. See Richard Maxwell Eaton, *Social History of the Deccan, 1300–1761* (Cambridge: Cambridge University Press, 2005), 105–28.

3. Quoted in Robert L. Irick, *Ch'ing Policy toward the Coolie Trade* (China: Chinese Materials Center, 1982), 11.

4. Quoted in Jacob Marcus, *The Jew in the Medieval World: A Sourcebook, 315–1791* (New York: JPS, 1938), 51–53.

5. Ibid., 53.

6. Ibid., 54.

7. Ibid.

8. Ibid.

9. Licence to Deport Black People (ca. January 1601), quoted in Paul L. Hughes and James F. Larkin, *Tudor Royal Proclamations* (New Haven: Yale University Press, 1969), 3: 221–22.

10. "Treaty of Westphalia," Cap. 70, The Avalon Project, Yale Law School, accessed April 21, 2013, www.avalon.law.yale.edu/17th_century/westphal.asp.

11. Quoted in Frances Gardiner Davenport, ed., *European Treaties Bearing on the History of the United States to 1648* (Washington: Carnegie Institution, 1917), 95–100.

12. Translated from Enrique Otte, *Cartas privadas de emigrantes de Indias, 1540–1616* (Seville, 1988), 81, in Kenneth Mills and William B. Taylor, eds., *Colonial Spanish America: A Documentary History* (Wilmington, DE: Scholarly Resources, 1998), 106–7.

13. Quoted in James Lockhard and Enrique Otte, eds., *Letters and People of the Spanish Indies: Sixteenth Century* (Cambridge: Cambridge University Press, 1976), 22: 136–37.

14. Ibid., 137–38.

15. Quoted in Albert Cook Myers, ed., *Narratives of Early Pennsylvania, West New Jersey, and Delaware, 1630–1707* (New York: Charles Scribner's Sons, 1912), 392–99.

16. Richard Frethorne, letters of March 20, 1623, and April 2–3, 1623, in Susan Kingsbury, ed., *Records of the Virginia Company of London* (Washington, DC: Government Printing Office, 1935), 4: 58–62.

17. Ibid.

18. Gottlieb Mittelberger, *Journey to Pennsylvania*, trans. Karl Theo. Eben (Philadelphia: John J. McVey, 1898), 19–271.

19. Ibid.

20. William Hawkins, *Hawkins' Voyages during the Reigns of Henry VIII, Queen Elizabeth, and James I*, ed. Clements R. Markham (New York: B. Franklin, 1970), 404.

21. Court Minutes, January 27, 1614, and February 4, 1614, in Great Britain, Public Record Office, *Calendar of State Papers, Colonial Series*, ed. W. Noel Sainsbury et al. (London: Public Record Office, 1860–1926), 2: 273–77; 3: 120.

22. See Jonathan D. Spence, *The Question of Hu* (New York: Vintage, 1989).

23. Cited in David J. Lu, ed., *Japan, A Documentary History* (Armonk, NY: M. E. Sharpe, 1997), 221.

## CHAPTER 4

1. Ancona Robin John, letter, August 17, 1774, quoted in Randy J. Sparks, *Two Princes of Calabar* (Cambridge: Harvard University Press, 2004), 85–86.

2. "Slaves' Appeal to Thomas Gage, Royal Governor of Massachusetts," May 25, 1774, quoted in *Modern History Sourcebook*, Fordham University, accessed April 22, 2013, www.fordham.edu/halsall/mod/1774slavesappeal.asp.

3. See Vincent Carretta, *Equiano, the African* (Athens: University of Georgia Press, 2005). Equiano's place of birth is uncertain, but his accurate personal accounts of slavery remain powerful.

4. Olaudah Equiano, *Interesting Narrative of the Life of Olaudah Equiano* (London: Author, 1794 edition), 193.

5. Olaudah Equiano, Petition to Queen Charlotte, March 21, 1788, in ibid., 352.

6. Quoted in F. M. Anderson, ed., *Constitutions and Other Select Documents Illustrative of the History of France, 1789–1907* (Minneapolis: H. W. Wilson, 1908), 184–85.

7. Dean Mahomet [sic], *Travels of Dean Mahomet*, ed. Michael H. Fisher (Berkeley: University of California Press, 1997), 42.

8. *Diario de la Habana* (December 6, 1847), quoted in Robert L. Irick, *Ch'ing Policy toward the Coolie Trade* (China: Chinese Materials Center, 1982), 1.

9. Testimony, quoted in ibid., 33–35.

10. Simón Bolívar, "An Address of Bolivar at the Congress of Angostura (February 15, 1819)," *Modern History Sourcebook*, Fordham University, accessed April 22, 2013, www.fordham.edu/halsall/mod/1819bolivar.asp.

11. "Convention for the Mutual Abolition of the Droit d'Aubaine and Taxes on Emigration Between the United States of America and his Majesty the King of Bavaria (January 21, 1845)," The Avalon Project, Yale Law School, accessed April 21, 2013, avalon.law.yale.edu/19th_century/bav1845.asp

12. "Bulletin of the Superintendent of the Census for 1890," quoted in Frederick Jackson Turner, *Frontier in American History* (New York: Henry Holt, 1921), 39.

13. *Life of Ma-Ka-Tai-Me-She-Kia-Kiak or Black Hawk . . . Dictated by Himself*, trans. Antoine Leclair, ed. Milo Milton Quaife (Chicago: Lakeland Press, 1916), 48, 106, 167.

14. Quoted in G. M. Theal, *Records of Southeastern Africa* (Cape Town: Government of Cape Town, 1898–1903), in *Modern History Sourcebook*, Fordham University, accessed April 22, 2013, www.fordham.edu/halsall/mod/1858basuto.asp.

15. *Memoirs of Catherine the Great*, trans. Mark Cruse and Hilde Hoogenbom (New York: Modern Library, 2005), 17, 26.

16. Ibid., 31–32.

17. Esper Ookhtomsky [Ukhtomskii], *Travels in the East of Nicholas II*, trans. R. Goodlet (Westminster: A. Constable, 1896), 2: 142–43, 444–46.

18. David J. Lu, *Japan: A Documentary History* (Armonk, NY: M. E. Sharpe, 1997), 308.

19. Article 22, Japan, *Constitution* (Baltimore, MD: Johns Hopkins University, 1889), 14.

20. Emma Lazarus, "The New Colossus," Liberty State Park, accessed April 23, 2013, www.libertystatepark.com/emma.htm.

21. "Naturalization Act of 1790," Library of Congress, accessed April 23, 2013, www.memory.loc.gov

22. "Chinese Exclusion Act of 1882," Our Documents Initiative, accessed April 23, 2013, www.ourdocuments.gov.

### CHAPTER 5

1. Anonymous report, death of N'Tchoréré, Archives Nationales, Service Historique de l'Armee, Chateau de Vincennes, 34N/1081, quoted in Myron Echenberg, "Morts Pour la France," *Journal of African History* 26, no. 4 (1985): 369–70.

2. "Karl Muffler," Immigration Museum, Victoria, Australia, accessed April 24, 2013, museumvictoria.com.au/discoverycentre/websites-mini/karl-muffler.

3. United Nations, "Convention on the Prevention and Punishment of the Crime of Genocide" (December 9, 1948), Article 2, accessed April 24, 2013, untreaty.un.org/cod/avl/ha/cppcg/cppcg.html.

4. Quoted in Emmett J. Scott, "Letters of Negro Migrants of 1916–1918," *Journal of Negro History* 4, no. 3 (July 1919): 317.

5. Ho Chi Minh, *Reminiscences*, quoted in William J. Duiker, *Ho Chi Minh* (New York: Hyperion, 2000), 49.

6. League of Nations, *Convention on Certain Questions Relating to the Conflict of Nationality Law*, April 13, 1930, League of Nations, Treaty Series, vol. 179, 89, no. 4137, Refworld, accessed April 24, 2013, www.unhcr.org/refworld/docid/3ae6b3b00.html.

7. United Nations General Assembly, *Universal Declaration of Human Rights*, December 10, 1948, 217 A (III), Article 13: 1, 2, Refworld, accessed April 24, 2013, www.unhcr.org/refworld/docid/3ae6b3712c.html.

8. Pseudonym, interviewed by Michael B. Griffiths, "Lamb Buddha's Migrant Workers: Self-Assertion on China's Urban Fringe," *Journal of Current Chinese Affairs* 39, no. 2 (2010): 26–27.

9. Ibid., 11.

10. United Nations General Assembly resolution 429(V), December 14, 1950, expanded in resolution 2198 (XXI) December 16, 1967, Refworld, accessed April 23, 2013 www.unhcr.org/refworld/docid/3b00f08a27.html and www.unhcr.org/refworld/docid/3b00f1cc50.html.

11. United Nations High Commissioner for Refugees, accessed April 24, 2013, www.unhcr.org/pages/49c3646c2.html.

12. United Nations High Commissioner for Refugees, *Global Trends 2011: A Year of Crisis*, accessed April 24, 2013, http://www.unhcr.org/4fd6f87f9.html.
13. Treaty on European Union, 92/C 191/01, Article 8a, 1, accessed April 24, 2013, eur-lex .europa.eu/en/treaties/dat/11992M/htm/11992M.html#0001000001.
14. The European Union continues to expand with Croatia (July 2013) and official Candidate Countries: Iceland, Montenegro, Serbia, the Former Yugoslav Republic of Macedonia, and Turkey.

# Further Reading

**PREFACE: MIGRATION IN WORLD HISTORY AND AS WORLD HISTORY**

Hreinsson, Vidar, ed. *The Complete Sagas of Icelanders*. 5 vols. Reykjavik: Leifur Eiriksson, 1997.

King, Russell, ed. *Atlas of Human Migration*. London: Marshall Editions, 2007.

Smith, Bonnie G., ed. *Oxford Encyclopedia of Women in World History*. New York: Oxford University Press, 2008.

**CHAPTER ONE: EARLIEST HUMAN MIGRATIONS, CA. 200,000 BCE TO 600 CE**

Heather, Peter. *Empires and Barbarians: The Fall of Rome and the Birth of Europe*. Oxford: Oxford University Press, 2010.

Polosmak, Natalya. "A Mummy Unearthed from the Pastures of Heaven." *National Geographic Magazine* 16, no. 4 (October 1994): 80–103.

Strudwick, Nigel C., and Ronald J. Leprohon. *Texts from the Pyramid Age*. Leiden: Brill, 2005.

Tattersall, Ian. *The World from Beginnings to 4000 BCE*. New York: Oxford University Press, 2008.

**CHAPTER TWO: MIXING AND CLASHING MIGRATIONS, 600 CE TO 1450**

Barfield, Thomas J. *Perilous Frontier: Nomadic Empires and China 221 BC to AD 1757*. Cambridge: Blackwell, 1989.

Davidson, H. R. Ellis. *Viking Road to Byzantium*. London: George Allen & Unwin, 1976.

Eaton, Richard Maxwell. *Islamic History as Global History*. Washington, DC: American Historical Association, 1990.

Ratchnevsky, Paul. *Genghis Khan, His Life and Legacy*, tr. Thomas Haining. Oxford: Blackwell, 1992.

Sturluson, Snorri. *King Harald's Saga: Harald Hardadi of Norway*, tr. Magnus Magnusson and Hermann Palsson. Baltimore, MD: Penguin, 1966.

**CHAPTER THREE: MIGRATIONS START TO RECONNECT THE WORLD, 1450 TO 1750**

Brown, Kathleen. *Good Wives, Nasty Wenches, and Anxious Patriarchs: Gender, Race, and Power in Colonial Virginia*. Chapel Hill: University of North Carolina Press, 1996.

Eaton, Richard Maxwell. *Social History of the Deccan, 1300–1761*. Cambridge: Cambridge University Press, 2005.

Gordon, Stewart. *When Asia Was the World*. Cambridge: Da Capo, 2008.

Howe, K. R. *Quest for Origins: Who First Discovered and Settled the Pacific Islands?* Honolulu: University of Hawai'i Press, 2003.

Salisbury, Neal. "Squanto: Last of the Patuxets." In *Struggle and Survival in Colonial America*, edited by David G. Sweet and Gary B. Nash, 228–44. Berkeley: University of California Press, 1981.

Spence, Jonathan D. *The Question of Hu*. New York: Vintage, 1989.

## CHAPTER FOUR: NATIONAL AND INTERNATIONAL MIGRATIONS, 1750 TO 1914

Byron, Reginald. *Irish America*. Oxford: Clarendon, 1999.

Curtin, Philip D. *Cross-cultural Trade in World History*. Cambridge: Cambridge University Press, 1984.

Fryer, Peter. *Staying Power: The History of Black People in Britain*. London: Pluto, 1984.

Lucassen, Jan, Leo Lucassen, and Patrick Manning, eds. *Migration History in World History: Multidisciplinary Approaches*. Leiden: Brill, 2010.

Rediker, Marcus. *Slave Ship: A Human History*. New York: Viking, 2007.

Wallerstein, Immanuel. *The Modern World-System*. 3 vols. New York: Academic, 1974–89.

## CHAPTER FIVE: MIGRATIONS IN THE AGE OF GLOBALIZATION, 1914 TO THE PRESENT

Flanders, Stephen A. *Atlas of American Migration*. New York: Facts on File, 1998.

Green, Nancy L., and François Weil, eds. *Citizenship and Those Who Leave: The Politics of Emigration and Expatriation*. Urbana: University of Illinois Press, 2007.

Hoerder, Dirk. *Cultures in Contact: World Migrations in the Second Millennium*. Durham, NC: Duke University Press, 2002.

Killingray, David. "African Voices from Two World Wars." *Historical Research* 74, no. 186 (November 2001): 425–43.

Koser, Khalid. *International Migration: A Very Short Introduction*. Oxford: Oxford University Press, 2007.

Pieke, Frank N. "Immigrant China." *Modern China* 38, no. 1 (2012): 40–77.

Reid, Richard J. *History of Modern Africa: 1800 to the Present*. Malden, MA: Wiley-Blackwell, 2012.

Stearns, Peter N. *Cultures in Motion: Mapping Key Contacts and Their Imprints in World History*. New Haven: Yale University Press, 2001.

# Websites

**Cobh Heritage Centre, Cork, Ireland**
*www.cobhheritage.com*
Emigration greatly affected many nations. This website and museum commemorate and document the histories of the millions of people who left Ireland and migrated across the globe.

**Fordham University's Internet History Sourcebooks Project**
*www.fordham.edu/Halsall/index.asp*
This project, edited by Paul Halsall, provides access to extensive primary source material from ancient to modern times for much of the world. Since migration history is the core of world history, these documents enable us to understand specific examples of migration from the perspective of people at the time.

**The Immigration History Research Center, University of Minnesota**
*www.ihrc.umn.edu*
This center promotes interdisciplinary research on international migration, develops archives documenting immigrant and refugee life, especially in the United States, and makes specialized scholarship accessible to students, teachers, and the public. The website provides finding aids, studies, and source material for students.

**The Immigration Museum, Melbourne, Australia**
*http://museumvictoria.com.au/ immigrationmuseum/*
Many nations celebrate their immigrants, providing personal stories and artifacts about their histories. This museum and its website provide engaging moving images, individual stories, and memorabilia for immigrants to Victoria, Australia.

**Moving Here, 200 Years of Migration in England**
*www.movinghere.org.uk*
This website makes available the histories and experiences of some of the diverse immigrants to England since 1800. The Moving Here Project shows how people entered English society and the continued significance of their respective ethnic groups in multicultural Britain today.

**Online Community on Migration and Integration—Building Inclusive Societies (IBIS)**
*www.unaoc.org/ibis*
The United Nations Alliance of Civilizations and the International Organization for Migration jointly created this international organization to reinforce efforts to harmonize the coexistence between newcomers and host communities, to improve social cohesion and intercultural relations, and to add complexity to debates around migration. The website includes extensive information about, and for, international migrants today.

**South Tyrol Museum of Archaeology, Bolzano, Italy**
*www.iceman.it*
This Italian museum features the growing scientific research on Ötzi, the iceman whose corpse and artifacts date to Neolithic times. The website reveals the many scientific methods of reconstructing the life and context of this fourth-century BCE migrant found in the Alps of Europe.

**The Statue of Liberty Ellis Island Foundation, Inc.**
*www.ellisisland.org*
   This foundation provides a museum and website that feature the experiences of the twenty million immigrants who entered the United States through Ellis Island (1892–1924). The website provides access to historical photographs and a searchable database of individual immigrants.

**The United Nations High Commissioner of Refugees**
*www.unhcr.org*
   The UN General Assembly created the UNHCR in 1950 to lead and coordinate international action to protect refugees and resolve refugee problems worldwide. Its primary purpose is to safeguard the rights and well-being of refugees. The website provides extensive documentation about today's international refugees.

**Voyages: The Trans-Atlantic Slave Trade Database**
*www.slavevoyages.org*
   This project's website provides searchable information about nearly 35,000 trans-Atlantic slaving voyages.

# NEW OXFORD WORLD HISTORY

The
New
Oxford
World
History

## GENERAL EDITORS

The New Oxford World History provides a comprehensive, synthetic treatment of the "new world history" from chronological, thematic, and geographical perspectives, allowing readers to access the world's complex history from a variety of conceptual, narrative, and analytical viewpoints as it fits their interests.

**Michael H. Fisher** holds the Robert S. Danforth Chair in History at Oberlin College. He has published many books and articles about migrations, primarily those of Asians and Europeans. His most recent book, *The Inordinately Strange Life of Dyce Sombre: Victorian Anglo Indian M.P. and Chancery 'Lunatic'* (2010), traces the life of a subject of the late Mughal Empire who emigrated to Britain and became the first Asian in the British Parliament, as well as a putative lunatic. Some of Fisher's earlier books about migrants include *Visions of Mughal India: An Anthology of European Travel Writing* (2007), *Counterflows to Colonialism: Indian Travellers and Settlers in Britain, 1600–1857* (2006), and *The First Indian Author in English: Dean Mahomed (1759–1851) in India, Ireland, and England* (2000).

# Index

slavery, 15, 18–19, 39, 55–57, 62; in Americas, 49, 67, 86, 100, 127; in Europe, 23–25, 74, 108; in Islam, 25, 34–35, 46, 51–53, 55; international trade, 66, 73–79, 83–84, 89, 103

Slavs, 23–25, 39–40, 57, 95–97, 108

Slovakia, 121

Slovenia, 115, 121

sojourners, 54, 71, 83–86, 109–15. *See also* return-migration

sons of the soil, nativist politics, 122. *See also* state policies

South Africa, 3–4, 92, 94–95, 113, 128; immigration, 86, 99, 101; Khoisan, 4, 71, 94

South America, 8, 11, 77, 81, 85. *See also* by individual nation

South Asia, 18, 22, 34, 55, 112. *See also* by individual nation

South Korea, 112. *See also* Koreans

South Sudan, 120

South Vietnam, 111. *See also* Vietnam

Southeast Asia, 5–7, 22, 33–36, 63; immigration, 12, 58, 81, 84. *See also* by individual nation

Spain, 31, 35, 48, 121, 127; emigration, 23, 60–65, 76, 83–85, 123; immigration, 25, 69

Sri Lanka, 22, 84, 110

state policies, 49, 73, 95, 108, 127; international organizations, 119–23, 128; nation-states, xiii, 79, 102, 113–14, 119–20; naturalization, 87, 100, 123. *See also* by individual nation

steppes, 16–18, 24–25, 50–51, 53–55, 59. *See also* by individual nation

sub-Saharan Africa, 11, 25–26, 32, 73, 86; immigration, 102. *See also* by individual nation

Sudan, 23, 105, 109, 120

Suez Canal, 86

Sufis, 30, 33, 53–54. *See also* Muslims

Sumatra, 6–7

Sumeria, 13–15. *See also* Iraq

Sunda, 6–7. *See also* Southeast Asia

Sweden, 66, 121. *See also* Scandinavia

swidden, 9, 33, 48

Switzerland, 112, 121

Syria, 28–31, 46–47, 106, 113–14, 119

Tahiti, 122. *See also* Pacific Ocean

Taiwan, 12, 99, 116, 118. *See also* China

Tanzania, 110

Tatars (Tartars), 41–43, 53–54, 57, 107

temporarily immigrant workers, 119–20. *See also* state policies

Texas, 90

Thailand, 120

Thirty Years' War, 61, 127. *See also* Europe, religion

Tibet, 26, 116. *See also* China

Timur, 54–55

Tordesillas, Treaty of, 63. *See also* Portugal, Spain

transhumant migration, 9, 41

transportation of criminals, 69, 80–81, 127. *See also* Britain

Tuareg, 32. *See also* Berbers

Tunisia, 25, 30–31, 120

Turkish Republic, 22, 106, 114, 120, 133

Turks, 34–35, 45, 50–55, 57, 120. *See also* Central Asia, Ottoman Empire

Tutsi, 109

Uganda, 110

Ukraine, 40, 53, 57, 96. *See also* Union of Soviet Socialist Republics

Underground Railway, 79. *See also* African Americans, United States

undocumented immigrants. *See* international migration

Union of Soviet Socialist Republics (USSR), 106–7, 114–15. *See also* Russia

United Kingdom. *See* Britain

United Nations, 108, 112–14, 118–20, 128; United Nations High Commissioner for Refugees, 119–20, 128; United Nations Relief and Works Agency, 113 (*see also* Palestinians)

United States, 84–93, 98–102, 119, 122–23, 125; African immigration, 64, 74–79, 109–10, 120; Asian immigration, 84, 101; European immigration, 62, 68–69, 81, 88–89; state policies, 59, 73, 107–112. *See also* Amerindians

Universal Declaration of Human Rights, 114, 119

urbanization, 58, 62, 90, 106–9, 117–18

Uruk, 14–15. *See also* Iraq

Utah, 90

Uzbeks, 50, 54, 57. *See also* Central Asia

Vandals, 25. *See also* Germans

Varangians, 40. *See also* Russia, Scandinavia

Venezuela, 85

Venice, 41, 53, 62

Vermont, 79

Vietnam, 43, 80, 110–11, 117–18, 120

Vikings, xi, 37–38. *See also* Scandinavia

Vinland, xi–xii

Virginia, 67, 70, 75–76

Western Sahara, 120

Westphalia, Treaty of, 61, 127. *See also* nation-state

white settler colonies, 62, 66. *See also* Britain, France
World Trade Organization, 112, 118
World War I, 19, 103–6, 109, 114, 128
World War II, 103, 105–13, 116, 128

Xiongnu, 16, 25

Y-chromosome. *See* genetic markers
Yemen, 23. *See also* Arabia
Yugoslavia, 52, 106–9, 114–16, 121, 133

Zanzibar, 110
Zapotec, 13. *See also* Mexico
Zaragoza, Treaty of, 63. *See also* Portugal, Spain
Zimbabwe, 73, 110, 113
Zulu, 92. *See also* South Africa

Printed in the USA/Agawam, MA
March 13, 2020

751982.001